Smart Church Management

A Quality Approach to Church Administration

By Patricia S. Lotich

Second Edition
Layout & Design by Resa Troyer for Resa Design, LLC
Patricia S. Lotich, 2012, 2015
ISBN - 978-0-9916450-1-5

Contents

Preface

God Has a Plan!

The Bible is very clear that God has a plan. The complexities of His plan are more than our human minds can comprehend but don't feel disillusioned. He has things under control. Sometimes, I sit in awe of how great God is. With all of our disobedience and operating outside of His plan, He still manages to move us toward His perfect will.

A major part of God's plan involves establishing churches that will train His people to do the ministry's work. With the great harvest just on the horizon, it's even more important for these churches to prepare and equip themselves to handle the multitudes of people who will flood their gates.

> "For as we have many members in one body, but all the members do not have the same function, so we, being many, are one body in Christ, and individually members of one another." Romans 12:4-5

As these training churches become established, people will prepare for what God has called them to do in the final days, and the church will be ready to handle the harvest.

The discipleship and ministry responsibility rests on the pastors, but the administrative side of the church rests on those who have the responsibility to manage church resources.

> "And God has appointed these in the church: first apostles, second prophets, third teachers, after that miracles, then

gifts of healings, helps, **administrations**, varieties of tongues." 1 Corinthians 12: 28

God gives the church resources—people, time, money—and people give their time to volunteer and tithe on their income. So managing God's resources is a huge responsibility that people should not take lightly. I wrote this book to help those with that responsibility.

CHAPTER 1

Church Mission

"Write the vision and make it plain on tablets, that he may run who reads it. For the vision is yet for an appointed time." Habakkuk 2:2-3

Mission, Vision, and Values

Every church has a part to play in God's plan and should take time in prayer to seek God's vision for their particular body of believers and work toward seeing that vision come to pass. The vision of each church supports God's "master plan" to influence a city or a nation. All the churches working together participate in wearing the tapestry of God's perfect plan around the world.

Before anyone can lead an organization, he or she needs to know why it exists, where it's going, and what steps to take to get there. This is why it's important to have a guiding mission, vision and values statement that articulates why the church exists, where it proposes to go, and what guiding principles will help direct its decision-making. Those who have the responsibility of overseeing the ministry, typically the church board, should participate in the development of the Mission, Vision, and Values statement.

The Vision Statement

A vision statement provides direction and a target for the church.

It's a tool to help the organization fulfill what God has called it to do. It's the bullseye!

The value of a church vision statement is that it gives church leadership, employees and congregants a shared goal. Every organization needs to understand where it's going before it can develop a strategic plan and map out steps for how to get there.

A church vision statement is typically two to three sentences that describe what the church hopes to become or achieve. Some organizations write paragraphs describing their vision, but I believe that the shorter the statement, the more likely employees, volunteers, and congregants can absorb it, memorize it, and explain it to others. It's important for the entire congregation to have a good understanding of what the church is trying to accomplish so that everyone can buy into and support the vision.

Steps to writing a church vision, mission, and values statement.

1. Gather church leadership

The church board and some senior church members or staff should write the church's Vision, Mission and Values statement.

Ideally, they do this in a retreat setting, such as a private room in a restaurant, a hotel conference room, or someone's home. It just needs to be a place without interruptions and distractions.

2. Solicit help from an objective facilitator

The beauty of the church is that God blesses churches with a wide variety of gifts, and a church congregation may have professionals available who are gifted at facilitation and are maybe interested in guiding a Vision, Mission, and Values session. If there is no one on the board or in the congregation who has this skill set, it may be worth investing in a couple of hours with a professional who can help. Regardless, the facilitator should drive the process and not the vision. An experienced facilitator will know how to do this.

3. Dream out loud

A visioning session is the "writing-on-tablet" process and attendees should pray before the session begins. The goal is to articulate God's will for the church. Once the session begins, I like working with whiteboards or flipcharts because I think a visual helps spark thoughts and ideas.

Depending on the number of people in the session, have the group break down into units of three to four people, provide each group with a flip chart, and have them discuss and answer the following questions:

- Who are we?
- Where does God want us to go?
- What do we want this church to look like?
- Where do we want to be 1, 5, 10 years from now?

As a group, create a newspaper headline about something the church has done/accomplished at some future point. This helps the group visualize the future.

4. Combine ideas and at the end of this session:

- Have all the units come back together and tell the group the thoughts and ideas they came up with.
- Use the entire group to pick the best and most consistent thoughts and ideas from each of the smaller groups and simply write the common words on a flipchart.
- Go around the room and allow all the participants to begin to add/subtract and formalize the sentence structure of the statement. Have a laptop available to use a thesaurus, dictionary, and encyclopedia/search engine as references.

5. Test the statement

Once they've written a couple of sentences, read them out loud to the group again and determine whether the entire group agrees that the statement reflects a common direction and describes a picture of an ideal future state of the church.

Following are some example vision statements:

Caterpillar: Be the global leader in customer value.

DuPont: The vision of DuPont is to be the world's most dynamic science company, creating sustainable solutions essential to a better, safer, and healthier life for people everywhere.

Heinz: Our vision, quite simply, is to be the world's premier food company, offering nutritious, superior tasting foods to people everywhere.

Sears: To be the preferred and most trusted resource for the products and services that enhance home and family life.

Avon: To be the company that best understands and satisfies the product, service, and self-fulfillment needs of women globally.

6. The Mission Statement

Once the vision statement is complete, do a similar exercise to come up with a mission statement. Remember a mission statement is a short description of "why" the organization exists.

Vision and mission statements are the cornerstone for decision-making.

I used to work for a pediatric hospital, and the mission was "We will do what is right for kids." It is simply stated, but it's very powerful in the boardroom. When challenged with difficult questions, senior leadership would ask, "Is this decision in the best interest of the kids we serve?"

This tool helps keep the organization focused on its priorities. A great book that can help teach your group how to simplify a message is *Made to Stick* by Chip and Dan Heath.

While in the same units, spend 20 to 30 minutes writing down descriptive words for why the church exists. After all the units write their ideas on the flipchart, have each unit present its ideas to the whole group.Using one flipchart, combine ideas and begin "wordsmithing" the ideas until the group creates a short phrase that reflects all ideas. Have all the units read the final statements and come to an agreement that the phrase truly reflects the church's mission and why it exists.

7. The Values Statement

Once there's a vision and mission statement, break the group into units again and allow them 20 minutes or so to list the organization's values (value = a principle, standard, or quality considered worthwhile or desirable). Remember, these will become shared values or principles the organization operates by.

- Once each unit has its list, have the members present it to the entire group.
- Combine ideas and refine them into one list. There are usually a lot of ideas that overlap (which is a good thing).
- Ideally, a list of values should be five to ten words. The goal is for people who align themselves with the organization to simply memorize the Vision, Mission, and Values statement. The more concise the better.

That wasn't so difficult, was it? Many churches and nonprofit organizations fail to come up with a vision, mission, and values statement because the process scares them, but with the right people in the room, they can do it in a few hours. Once they've written it, the strategic planning process can begin!

CHAPTER 2

Strategic Planning

"Commit your works to the Lord,"
And your thoughts will be established."
Proverbs 16:3

Strategic Planning

A strategic plan articulates the mission and vision and creates a road map for getting there. The written plan describes where the church is today and how it will fulfill God's vision for the church.

Strategic planning can be tedious. It takes a lot of time, thought, and prayer. The process typically takes weeks or even months, depending on how much time the committee can devote to it on a day-to-day basis. Board level members with senior leadership do the strategic planning.

The strategic planning process identifies *what* members need to do (vision and strategic plan), *how* to do it (organizational and departmental goals) and who will do it (employee and volunteer job descriptions). This structured process helps to ensure the vision implementation throughout the entire organization.

Developing the Plan

Strategic plans help to map out the steps, process, and timeline to get from the present state of the organization to the desired future state.

In order to do this, there are two different levels of planning required: short-term (3 to 6 months) and long- term (12 to 36 months).

It used to be that strategic plans were for anywhere from five to even ten years out, but as quickly as things change today, a three-year plan is probably as aggressive as you can get without needing to modify the plan along the way.

Strategic Planning Process

The first step identifies the outcome: where do you want to be in three years? Take some time to brainstorm or visualize what that future state looks like. For example, strategic objectives or outcomes may be things like building a Bible school, planting churches, sending missionaries to certain parts of the world, or developing worship leaders—anything that supports the church vision.

Next, create a timeline for completion of your objectives and determine how many weeks, months, or years it will realistically take to complete the objectives. This involves thinking through the high-level action steps needed to complete the tasks.

Example: Three-Year Strategic Plan

Three Year Strategic Objectives	**Year 1**	**Year 2**	**Year 3**
1. Reduce operating budget by 5 percent, from $1M to $950,000 by end of year 1.			
2. Grow volunteer base by 10 percent, from 100 to 110 by end of year 2.			
3. Grow church from 1200 to 1500 members by end of year 3.			
4. Plant church 50 miles from current church location by end of year 3.			

Once you've identified where you want to be (this should line up with the vision God has given your ministry), the next step is to start mapping out what it will take to get there.

For example, to plant a church, what are the steps you need to take, that is, identify church plant leader, identify new church location, decide on church model, transition plan for leader, timeline to new church opening, etc. This detailed planning works well in the format of an action plan.

An action plan is merely a written document outlining the objectives (goals), action steps, responsible person(s), possible team members, due date for each action step, and implementation status. Mapping this out creates a visual that's easy to see at a glance for what you need to do and by when.

Example: Strategic Objective Action Plan

Strategic Objective #4 Action Plan				
Strategic Objective	Action Steps	Responsible Person(s)	Due Date	Status
Plant church 50 miles from current church location by end of year 3.	Identify church plant leader.	Church board	June 15, 20XX Year 1	Completed
	Create timeline for new church opening.	Senior leadership	Dec 31, 20XX Year 1	Completed
	Create transition plan for new church leader.	Church board, senior leadership	June 30, 20XX Year 2	In progress
	Decide on church model.	Church board	Sept 30, 20XX Year 2	In progress
	Identify new church location.	Church board	Dec 31, 20XX Year 2	In progress
	Open new church.	Senior leadership	Sept 30, 20XX Year 3	In progress

As you create the action plan, you will identify objectives or steps that individual church departments need to take to support strategic objectives. As each department identifies its goals and objectives, it provides the information needed to write individual (or volunteer) job descriptions that support departmental goals, organizational goals, and, ultimately, the strategic plan.

This graphic shows how goals and accountability flow throughout the organization.

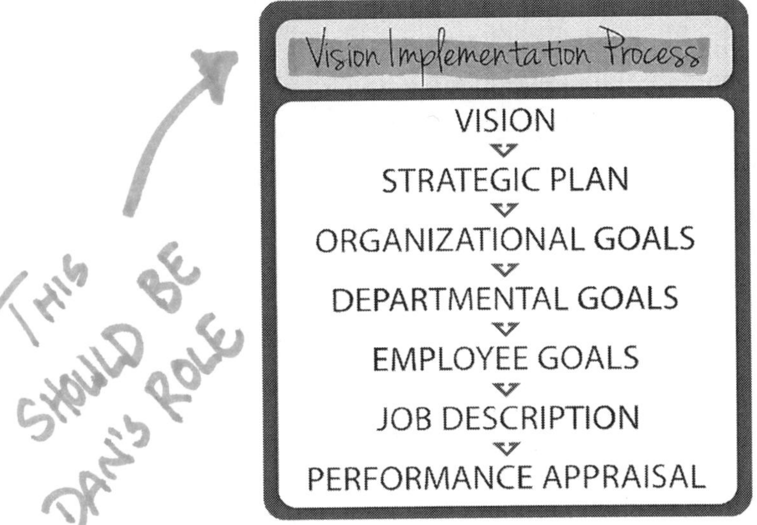

Vision Implementation Process

Organizational Goals

As the organization works toward accomplishing the strategic plan, there needs to be a structured process to take the organization from where it is to where it wants to be. Do this by developing annual organizational goals. Annual goals break long-term goals into bite-sized pieces. This provides the framework for accomplishing them in steps and stages rather than all at once, and it serves as a tool for performance monitoring.

Monitor performance by taking the goals down to the departmental and staff level and ensuring that what staff members are doing day-to-day lines up with the organization's vision and goals. It's easy for employees to get off track day-to-day, but this process will keep them focused on the organization's priorities.

Goals are important because they provide direction, clarify job roles, give employees something to strive for, and help make the vision attainable. Writing down your goals makes them more real and achievable because it allows you to see where you're going and what steps you must take to get there.

The structured process should include a cycle that begins with writing goals, communicating expectations, monitoring performance toward goals, and assessing performance and ends with the performance appraisal. This cycle repeats annually. Once the organization has some direction for the next twelve months, the leaders can delegate the organizational priorities to individual departments. This step ensures there's a person or a group of people with responsibility for goal completion.

SMART Goals

Part of the planning process is setting church goals. Write goals so they're measurable and are an outcome of the strategic planning process. Goals simply map out steps to achieve a strategic objective and do not need to be overly complicated. But, implementation of goals does require discipline and a commitment to follow through to completion.

I like to use the SMART goal model.

SMART Goals are:

Specific: Is the goal **specific** enough for clarity?
Measurable: Is there a way to **measure** the success of the goal?
Attainable: Is the goal truly **attainable?**
Realistic: Is the goal **realistically** written?
Timely: Is there a **timeline** associated with the goal to ensure a completion date?

Writing goals should include a discussion with the appropriate people and answer the questions:
Who (will do it)

What (needs to be done)
When (timeline for completion)
How (steps to get it done)

Answering these questions flushes out the specific details of the goal.

Church goals should tie in to the strategic plan and assignment responsibility, timeline, and action steps. As you can see in this goal document, each goal aligns with a strategic objective.

Example: Church Goals

Church 20XX Goals				
Goal	Strategic Objective	Responsibility	Due Date	Status
Reduce operating budget by 5 percent, from $1M to $950,000	#1	Ted Smith	June, 30, 20XX	Pending
Increase weekly volunteer participation by 10 percent (100 to 110)	#2	Kathy Thompson	December 31, 20XX	Pending
Increase weekly attendance 20 percent (500 to 600)	#3	Pastor Richardson	December 31, 20XX	Pending
Create church plant strategy and plan	#4	Pastor Richardson	October, 31, 20XX	Pending

Departmental Goals

Now let's take these annual goals and apply them at the department level. This requires assigning the goal to a specific department. For example, the volunteer department can handle the church goal of increasing volunteer participation by 10 percent.

Now let's look at one of these goals and create a goal document

Example: Department Goal Document

Volunteer Department 20XX Goals				
Goals	Steps	Responsibility	Due Date	Status
Increase volunteer participation by 10 percent (100 to 110) by December, 20XX	Research what percentage of core members are actively volunteering.	Kathy Thompson	May 12	Completed
	Develop volunteer recruitment campaign.	Dan Smith	June 1	Completed
	Organize volunteer fair.	Stacy Jones	July 1	Pending
	Process new volunteers.	Stacy Jones	Sept 1	Pending
	Assign new volunteers.	Stacy Jones	Oct 1	Pending
	Schedule new volunteers.	Stacy Jones	Nov 15	Pending
	Compare total volunteer numbers to original.	Kathy Thompson	Dec 15	Pending

Employee Goals

To ensure that the departments accomplish their goals, they need to delegate them to individual employees or volunteers. Do this by mapping the goals and steps the employee needs to take in order to accomplish the goals.

As you will note, these goals line up with individual departmental goals. This tool is very valuable during the annual performance appraisal process because it will determine whether the organization accomplished these goals, which were set at the beginning of the year, by the end of the year.

Now, we will take the previous departmental goal and break it down into steps for an employee or volunteer to accomplish.

Let's take it a step farther and create an employee (or volunteer) goal.

Example: Employee Goal Document

Stacy Jones 20XX Goals				
Goals	Steps	Responsibility	Due Date	Status
Organize volunteer fair	Schedule date on church calendar.	Stacy Jones	February 1	Completed
	Advertise fair in church bulletin, website, and announcement.	Stacy Jones	May 1	Completed
	Recruit representatives to answer questions the day of the fair.	Stacy Jones	May 1	Completed
	Gather volunteer information recruitment material.	Stacy Jones	June 1	Completed
	Develop plan for booth design and layout.	Stacy Jones	June 1	Pending
	Set up fair booths.	Stacy Jones	June 14	Pending
	Participate in fair.	Stacy Jones	June 15	Pending

As you will notice, Stacy takes the objective (goal) from the action steps in the (volunteer) departmental goal. This allows Kathy Thompson to assign responsibility to Stacy Jones for accomplishing this goal.

This document is for use when Stacy receives her review at her annual performance appraisal, which will demonstrate her goal completion. When Stacy completes her goal, it allows Kathy Thompson to accomplish her goal, which supports the global church goals.

Managers use the goal document as a guide throughout the year to reinforce deadlines outlined in the worksheet. In addition, managers incorporate employee goals into the performance appraisal process.

These examples demonstrate how simplified the process is, so hopefully, it will encourage you to take the time to create a goal document.

A church's ability to write and accomplish organizational goals is critical to implementing a strategic plan and ultimately achieving ministry objectives.

Employee Job Descriptions

Write job descriptions to reflect individual goals that support the departmental goals. Job descriptions should describe reporting relationships (this is to identify who the boss is). They should also list day-to-day job duty accountabilities that this person is responsible for doing. Review and update job descriptions annually (the performance appraisal is a good time to do this).

As you can see, in the highlighted line above, the responsibility of organizing the volunteer fair is part of the office assistant's job duties description. This provides a direct link between staff members' job duties, their department goals, and, ultimately, the global goals that support the strategic plan.

Example: Job Description

Job Title	Volunteer Office Assistant
Position reports to:	Manager, Volunteer Office
Salary range:	$XX,000–$XX,000
Employment status:	Full-time/Nonexempt
Position Overview	
Ensures volunteers receive support and professional and respectful treatment.	
Principal Accountabilities	
• Answers volunteer office phone and greets volunteers upon arrival. • Works with volunteer office manager to ensure efficient office operations. • Processes volunteer applications by entering information into volunteer database. • Runs and distributes volunteer reports for manager and volunteer supervisors. • Conducts background checks on volunteer applicants. • Tracks volunteer applications and notifies manager of any application holdup. • Takes responsibility for maintaining volunteer files and ensures all necessary documentation is in every file. This includes performing an annual file audit to ensure all files are compliant with audit guidelines. • Makes reference check phone calls. • Informs manager of potential volunteer issues. • Calls and recruits volunteers to help with special events or activities. • Organizes and submits applications to approval committee. • Performs volunteer office mailings. • **Organizes volunteer fair.** • Works with volunteer office manager to develop and maintain accurate volunteer job descriptions. • Works with volunteer office manager to develop annual volunteer office goals. • Takes responsibility for completion of annual goals. • Performs other duties the volunteer office manager requests.	

CHAPTER 3

Managing Performance

"Do not withhold good from those to whom it is due,
when it is in the power of your hand to do so."
Proverbs 3:27

Managing Employee Performance

Hold all church staff accountable for their job duties. Accountability means, "subject to giving an account; answerable." Goals are only as effective as the person who has responsibility for completing them. When church staffs aren't held accountable for achieving objectives, it can hinder strategic plan implementation.

In order to hold staff accountable for their responsibilities, a structured performance management process is necessary. Performance management is merely communicating expectations and managing the performance of employees. Unfortunately, not all employees have the self-motivation to get things done with accuracy and in a timely manner. Anyone who has ever managed people knows that some employees are self-starters while others need managing.

So what are the tricks to managing staff performance?

Setting Clear Performance Expectations

One of the biggest mistakes managers make is not communicating clear expectations to employees. I have counseled countless managers who voice frustration when employees don't perform to the desired level. My first question is: How did you communicate expectations to the employee? More times than not, the manager admits an informal communication process that doesn't include a lot of detail.

Communicating Clear Expectations

The manager is responsible for articulating expectations in a goal document and allowing the employee to ask clarifying questions. This should be an open two-way conversation that makes the expectations clear.

As the illustration below suggests, the more time a manager spends with an employee on the front end (orientation to job and clarification of expectations), the less time the manager needs to spend with the employee on the back end. Clear communication that allows for clarification and questions minimizes issues later in the process.

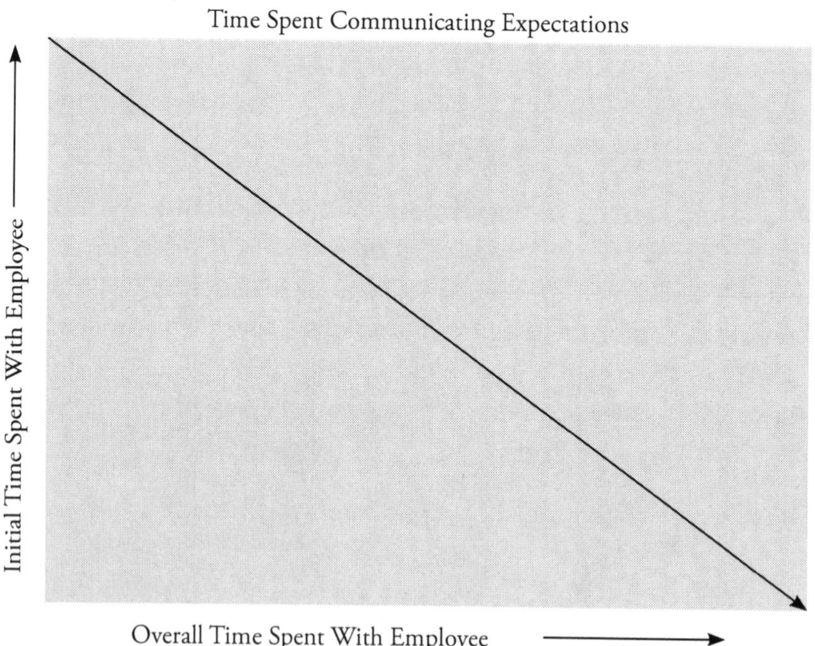

Monitoring Progress Toward Goals

Once the manager shares expectations with the employee, the manager should follow up occasionally and ask the employee how things are going, finding out whether there are any questions and whether there are any barriers to completing goals.

Often, internal systems, processes, and sometimes people hinder an employee's ability to achieve goals. The manager needs to know about this, so he or she can help remove anything that might interfere with completing the goal.

Documenting Conversations

So many things compete for a manager's attention, and that sometimes makes it difficult to remember conversations with employees. Creating a structured note-taking process helps ensure there's a history of important staff conversations.

Note-taking is a simple way to document employee performance conversations. Paragraphs of information aren't necessary, just enough to tickle your memory to have a conversation about it. Creating a system that works for you is the best approach.

Here's an example of a model I've used. If you use a planning calendar, you can keep a separate page for each employee in the back. On those pages simply jot down any significant incident or conversation that occurs with that employee. Make the following columns and fill them in after an employee conversation.

- Employee name
- Incident date
- Incident time
- Incident description
- Person(s) involved
- Action taken

Example: Note-Taking Log

Name	Date	Time	Incident Description	Persons Involved	Action Taken
Maggie Jones	Jan 3	11:00 am	Maggie did a great job by proactively preparing for the staff presentation.	Maggie Jones	Stopped by Maggie's desk and thanked her for taking care of the presentation.
	Feb 9	9:00 am	Maggie arrived 45 minutes late for work.	Maggie	Stopped by Maggie's desk and reminded her of the tardy policy.
	April 6	1:00 pm	Noticed that the quarterly board report had three typos.	Maggie	Pointed out typos and coached Maggie on proofing techniques.
	June 12	6:00 pm	Maggie stayed late without being asked to finish report for John.	Maggie	Thanked Maggie for going above and beyond to finish the report.

This example log shows how a manager can document employee conversations about both positive and negative behavior. This demonstrates that the employee is receiving continual feedback that helps him or her to better understand the behavior boundaries, and it reinforces positive behavior.

This log will also help when the manager prepares the employee performance appraisal form.

All the information on this log will help create an objective performance appraisal for the prior 12 months, and it will allow for an honest, objective, factual, and unbiased conversation with the employee.

This kind of structured annual process works to celebrate employee successes and helps to correct behaviors that may have veered off course. This approach to note-taking may seem like extra work, but it's well worth the time to have lots of data and be prepared for the annual evaluations. Developing employees is one of the most rewarding aspects of managing people, and it is a big responsibility the manager shouldn't take lightly.

The Performance Management Cycle

Creating a structured, predictable cycle for managing performance helps to get things done and supports completion of annual goals.

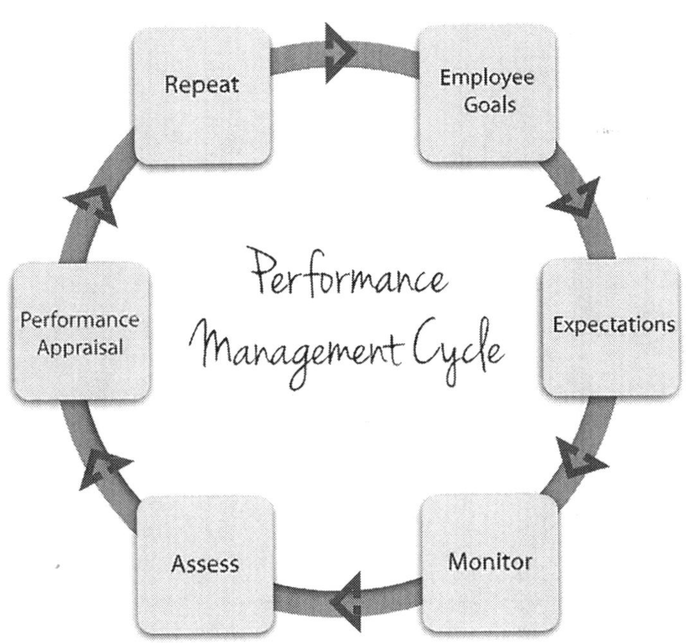

Expectations

It's important to explain goals and ensure employees understand what the supervisor expects of them. The best way to do this is to have the employee involved in the goal development process. Without employee involvement, buy-in to the goal can be a challenge.

Doing an assessment on a regular basis (several times a year) eliminates the last-minute gathering of information at performance appraisal time.

Why Do Performance Appraisals?

Churches use the performance appraisal process to help manage employee performance and achievement of ministry goals. It's important to have well-trained church managers and a structured process to document church employee performance and give performance appraisals.

A well-done performance appraisal process can be a positive experience for the employee and help the employee see how he or she contributes to organizational goals. If not done well, the performance appraisal can be a very stressful time and one of the most difficult conversations of the year.

The performance appraisal process should be a time to reflect on the past year and celebrate successes. The manager should also use it as a time to correct course if an employee has gotten off track. Reinforcing the positive and celebrating the successes can influence future positive behavior.

Statistics show that an estimated 40 percent of workers never receive performance evaluations. And for the 60 percent of the workers who do, the supervisor does poorly. Wow, what a scary thing!

The fact is that employees want and need to know whether they're doing a good job. A formal performance appraisal process forces managers to communicate both good and bad performance results to the employees.

Goals don't just happen; they need structured systems and processes, and the performance appraisal process is an important part of the cycle.

Example: Church Staff Performance Appraisal

The first step in creating an employee performance appraisal form is to identify those things (dimension measures) needed to assess the employee. Use the values statement and guiding principles as well as those employee characteristics that are important to a successful performance.

For instance, a church value is teamwork or customer service, so the evaluation measures a successful performance as an employee's ability to work with others, communicate well, or possess certain job skills.

Examples of common dimension measures of performance are teamwork, communication, attendance, job knowledge, and goal completion. These dimensions are church-specific and globally a part of the strategic planning process.

Each of the measures should have a description that's clear and understandable for the employee. For example:

Teamwork: Employee values team interactions and works effectively with others. The employee is a team player and helps encourage and orient new team members. Employee can balance personal effort and project team effort.

Communication: Employee communicates professionally with others and shares thoughts and ideas appropriately. Listens to others, asks clarifying questions, and controls emotions under pressure.

Customer focus: Employee understands who the customers are and actively responds to customer needs and adheres to ministry service standards.

Attendance and punctuality: Employee shows up for work at assigned time and provides ample notice when unable to come to work. Uses designated time off forms to request time away from job.

Job knowledge: Employee understands every aspect of job tasks and responsibilities and proactively updates job skills. Employee offers assistance to help others improve skills.

Goal completion: Employee completed annual goals as assigned.

Okay, now let's come up with a scale to measure these dimensions. There are different schools of thought on scaling. Some prefer a five-point scale, but others use a ten-point scale because it's a slightly tighter measure.

The rating scale determines the way you word the description of the measurement dimension.

Common scales are:

- Strongly Disagree – Agree – Strongly Agree
- Never – Sometimes – Always
- Of No Importance at All – Moderately Important – Extremely Important
- Dissatisfied – Satisfied – Extremely Satisfied

Ok, now let's create these dimensions on a measurement scale in an example performance appraisal form. This form incorporates both the employee self-assessment as well as the manager's assessment of the employee.

Example: Performance Appraisal

ABC Community Church
20XX Performance Appraisal

Employee Name: ________________________
Department: ___________________________
Please check the box that best describes frequency of performance measure.

Customer Focus: Employee understands who his/her customers are and proactively responds to customer needs. Employee adheres to ministry service standards with every customer contact.					
	Never 1	2	Sometimes 3	4	Always 5
Employee Self-Assessment					
Employee Comments					
Manager Assessment					
Manager Comments					
Teamwork: Employee values team interaction and works effectively with others. Is a team player and helps encourage and orient new team members. Is able to balance personal effort with project team effort.					
	Never 1	2	Sometimes 3	4	Always 5
Employee Self-Assessment					
Employee Comments					
Manager Assessment					
Manager Comments					
Job knowledge: Employee understands every aspect of job task and responsibilities and proactively updates job skills. Offers assistance to help others improve job skills.					
	Never 1	2	Sometimes 3	4	Always 5
Employee Self-Assessment					
Employee Comments					
Manager Assessment					
Manager Comments					
Communication: Employee comunicates professionally with others in print and shares thoughts and ideas appropriately. Listen to others and ask questions for clarity. Controls emotions under pressure.					
	Never 1	2	Sometimes 3	4	Always 5
Employee Self-Assessment					
Employee Comments					
Manager Assessment					
Manager Comments					

Performance Appraisal Delivery

Since we're all human, it's common for us to make "errors" when assessing employee performance. These errors reflect our unconscious biases toward the employee and can give an employee an advantage or disadvantage over others in the peer group.

Rater errors as described in *Human Resource Strategy* by Dreher and Dougherty reflect our imperfect judgment of others. It's for this reason it's important to understand these biases and take them into consideration when preparing a performance appraisal document.

According to the authors, "A barrier to the accuracy and credibility of performance measures is posed by a number of rater errors, perceptual biases, and other sources of distortion in performance ratings." There are six common rater errors that managers make when assessing performance. Understanding what these errors are can help keep managers from falling victim to them.

So what are the six rater errors?

Halo Effect

The Halo effect happens when a rater's overall positive or negative impression of an individual employee leads to rating him or her the same across all rating dimensions.

This happens when a manager really likes or dislikes an employee and allows personal feelings about this employee to influence performance ratings.

Leniency Error

Leniency error refers to a rater's tendency to rate all employees at the positive end of the scale (leniency) or at the low end of the scale (negativity). This can happen when a manager overemphasizes either positive or negative behavior.

Central Tendency Error

Central tendency error refers to the rater's tendency to avoid making extreme judgments of employee performance, resulting in rating all employees in the middle part of a scale. This can happen either when a manager isn't comfortable with conflict and avoids low marks to avoid dealing with behavioral issues or when a manager intentionally forces all employees to the middle of the scale.

Recency Error

Recency error is the rater's tendency to allow more recent incidents (either effective or ineffective) of employee behavior to carry too much weight in evaluation of performance over an entire rating period.

This can be extreme on both ends of the spectrum.

Either an employee is just finishing a major project successfully or an employee may have had a negative incident right before the performance appraisal process, and it's in the forefront of the manager's thoughts about that employee. It's for this reason it's important to keep accurate records of performance throughout the year to refer to during performance appraisal time.

First Impression Error

First impression error is the rater's tendency to let his/her first impression of an employee's performance carry too much weight in evaluating a performance over an entire rating period. An example of this would be a new employee joining the organization and performing at high levels during the honeymoon period and then losing some of that initial momentum as time goes on.

Similar-to-me Error

Similar-to-me error means the rater's tendency is to rate employees seen as similar to themselves well. We can all relate to people who are like us, but we cannot let our ability to relate to someone influence our rating of the employee's performance.

The Performance Appraisal Conversation

Preparation for the performance appraisal is ongoing. A manager should always think about the process, and whenever he or she notices a problem with an employee's performance, mention it to the employee and make a note of it. At the same time, whenever an employee demonstrates a desired behavior or result, mention it to the employee and make a note of it.

Performance appraisals need to be *fair, pertinent, and comprehensive.* Treat all employees the same, and track and observe their behavior the same way. Terminology of observations and documented behavior should show no biases in the process.

Questions to ask yourself when completing the PA form:

- Would I have made the same note on a different employee?
- Are my observations the same, or am I overemphasizing a single event?
- Am I giving immediate feedback after I observe a problem so the employee has a chance to change his/her behavior and improve?

Keep the appraisal pertinent to how the employee performs the job and make it relevant to job expectations and established standards of work. It should be comprehensive in monitoring and observing behavior that tells a story about the employee throughout the entire performance period.

Document and file all unusual events that affect performance. It's also important to note a positive performance and major accomplishments in order to be fair and balanced. The positive notes are important for celebration of successes at the performance appraisal time. Documentation helps you to remember the details of the observation.

Use a third party occasionally to review your observations to help keep you focused and objective.

Performance Appraisal Preparation

When it's time to do the performance appraisal, determine what information to include and exclude in the final appraisal. Look for information that shows patterns in behavior. This is not a time to surprise the employee, which is why each time you make a note for the file the employee should know it.

It's important to block out time on your calendar to write the performance appraisal. A good rule of thumb is to allow at least one hour per employee to review the file, organize content, and write performance appraisals.

Take time to write and do an initial draft of the appraisal ahead of the deadline. Sleep on it, look at the draft again, and test it to make sure it's a comprehensive assessment that's pertinent and fair.

Take time to discuss the employee's performance with the second-level supervisor. This will help to ensure that you have no biases in your evaluation.

Schedule the performance appraisal at an appropriate time and a neutral location. Try to use a conference room; a manager's office can intimidate an employee.

When delivering the performance appraisal, make sure you have no interruptions. Have specific examples of effective and ineffective performance prepared and be ready to answer questions, if asked.

Performance Appraisal Discussion

When you begin the discussion, be sure to state the purpose of the appraisal and the process you'll use for the discussion.

Review the appraisal with the employee while probing for additional information, misunderstandings, or views that differ from yours. Once you finish the discussion, summarize it and have the employee sign the appraisal for the files.

Managers must be willing to commit significant amounts of time to performance management. A lack of clear performance expectations and detailed performance feedback are a major source of stress for employees. It's important to make sure the employee's job description reflects what's in the goals.

Finally, try to remember that most employees want to do a good job and it's the manager's responsibility to help them identify their boundaries and goals and to provide them with the necessary resources to accomplish them.

CHAPTER 4

Leadership

"Moreover you shall select from all the people able men, such as fear God, men of truth, hating covetousness; and place such over them to be rulers of thousands, rulers of hundreds, rulers of fifties, and rulers of tens."
Exodus 18:21

Leadership

Leadership means "the ability to lead; an act or instance of leading; guidance; direction." Leadership is about how we behave, communicate, and manage others. The term is used in many forms to describe many things, but it's ultimately the act of leading people in a certain direction. It requires followers before someone can lead.

Successful professionals demonstrate leadership characteristics while continuing on their own personal development journey. They are life learners and take pride in developing others and watching them grow. Managing a church staff is no different and requires managers and leaders who can influence how work gets accomplished. Strong leaders have certain traits and characteristics that affect their interactions with others.

> "Leaders are people who do the right thing; managers are people who do things right." Warren Bennis

10 Leadership Traits

1. Person of Influence

Leaders influence others to accomplish things. They help others see needs and then show them the path forward. Anyone can be a leader, even kids. Did your mom ever say, "She's a bad influence on you"? That means that person influences your thoughts and behavior. Positive influence is what we're going for.

Leaders often influence us even though we may not know it. The CEO of the hospital I worked for would walk down the hall and pick up trash if he saw it on the floor. This example naturally influenced employees to do the same. It was an unspoken but powerful way to influence others.

2. Big Picture Thinker

Leaders are big picture thinkers and can rise above the day-to-day and see things from a broad perspective. They can get people excited about where they're going and how to get there. People often get stuck in their own little corner of the world and need help seeing things from a bird's eye view.

Employees need to get out of their cubes and hear stories of how their work affects those whom the church is reaching. My pastor does a great job of providing employees and volunteers with testimonies of people whose lives the ministry has touched. This shows the person who cleans the bathroom that his or her work helps to influence the lives of others.

3. Believes the Best in People

Effective leaders always give others the benefit of the doubt ("a favorable judgment given in the absence of full evidence") and believe the best in people. A true leader first gathers all the facts before drawing final conclusions.

It's amazing how one-sided a situation can look and how very different it seems when you have all the information. My husband always says there are three sides to every story. Make sure you know all the facts before making judgments.

4. Others See Them as Credible

Leaders maintain credibility with those they lead, which means they do what they say, say what they mean, and can communicate honestly with others. Others quickly recognize when a leader's actions don't line up with his/her speech.

A leader's personal life is consistent with his professional life, and he's unchanged, no matter who's around. There have been so many sad examples of leaders who have fallen when they live double lives, and their integrity is not consistent in every area of their lives.

5. Teacher and Mentor

Leaders are gifted teachers and love to help others develop. They model leadership principles and help others to be credible people. They help employees identify growth opportunities and coach others on personal growth.

They're not afraid of delegating responsibility, and they enjoy seeing others develop. People who are smarter than they are don't threaten them, and they take pleasure in seeing others succeed. I always told my staff that I would know that I did a good job if I could walk out the door one day and know that things would go on as if I were still there. Pulling people up behind us is how we all grow.

6. Master Delegator

Leaders develop others and learn to delegate responsibilities. They do this by allowing others to make mistakes and helping them learn from those mistakes.

We learn best from making mistakes, and allowing others to gain knowledge from their own mistakes is an invaluable lesson. All of us have had a starting point in our professional development, and allowing others to learn through experiences helps them grow professionally and gain self-confidence.

7. Empowers Others

Leaders empower others and recognize that making front-line decisions and taking risks are part of the development and learning process. People need to feel comfortable taking risks, making decisions, and learning from their mistakes.

Establishing boundaries and allowing others to test decision-making and problem-solving not only helps with employee development but also takes the bottleneck out of addressing customer issues whether they're internal (employee to employee) or external (organization to customer). The most important aspect of this is not allowing the employees (or volunteers) to feel as if they're hanging out there by themselves.

Debriefing after a mistake and coaching them to think of what might have been a better approach is part of the learning process.

It is very much like parenting; sometimes you need to allow your kids to fall down and pick themselves back up. That's how they learn.

8. Team Player

Leaders are team players and work well with others to get things done. They operate out of a win-win philosophy and help others to collaborate and come to agreement in tasks. They're skilled at managing team dynamics and developing team cohesiveness. They do this by holding team members accountable for their actions and keeping them focused on the team goal.

9. Celebrates Successes

Effective leaders can recognize success and help their team celebrate those successes. This is a critical component in team function and development. Rewarding performance and celebrating successes help to keep team members engaged. Even celebrating small successes provides the motivation and fuel to go after the bigger targets. No success is too small to celebrate and can be as simple as a public acknowledgement of success!

10. Has Balanced Priorities

Leaders have a good understanding of their personal priorities and can keep all aspects of their lives balanced. They understand the importance of setting personal boundaries and giving family as much focus and attention as their professional responsibilities.

They unapologetically recognize that leadership is a marathon and not a sprint, and they understand the importance of pacing themselves so they don't run out of gas before the race is complete. This is difficult to do in today's fast-paced environment, but successful leaders know how to work faster and more efficiently to achieve this balance.

Ethics and Integrity in Business Practice

Any ministry's success builds on the trust of its congregants, volunteers, and the public. The best way to gain that trust is to demonstrate ethics and integrity in church operations, not because of legal requirements, but because it's the right thing to do.

The integrity of any organization affects all customer groups and every area of business operations, which is why incorporating ethics and integrity into the core fabric of the ministry is critical.

> "Do the right thing. It will gratify some people and astonish the rest." Mark Twain

Churches that operate with integrity do so intentionally and make it part of their culture and everyday practices. This culture of honesty and trust helps orient new employees to understand that operating with integrity is "the way things are done around here." Building integrity into the culture is the foundation for ethical practices. Churches that strive to do the right thing benefit by establishing a reputation for high ethical standards. It starts at the top and flows throughout the entire organization.

Accounting Practices

Transparency with finances is a basic expectation of congregants, volunteers, and employees. It serves no one when churches mismanage funds, whether it's intentional or accidental.

Careless accounting practices limit a ministry's ability to manage its financial resources and can threaten its tax-exempt status. Preparing a well-thought-out annual budget that supports the strategic plan can help manage and control spending.

Cash Handling

Good cash-handling policies and procedures are critical to ensure the safeguarding of church funds.

And yes, churches are just as susceptible to embezzlement as any other organization. The reason is unsupervised access to cash is simply too tempting for many people, particularly people with a financial need. And yes, Christians steal, and they steal from churches. It's the responsibility of church leadership to safeguard cash donations and cash assets.

Studies of fraud and embezzlement have shown that people with incentive (a need), rationalization (I deserve this), and the right opportunity (easy access) are candidates for embezzling funds. Good cash-handling procedures can help to protect the organization and the employee and prevent fraud.

Every church is different, and each has very specific needs when it comes to handling cash. Some churches only handle cash when counting weekly offerings, but other churches handle cash at church events, the lobby coffee shop, or the church bookstore.

The best way to prevent easy access is to ensure more than one person handles the cash. Two-person cash-handling policies ensure safe handling and eliminate the temptation to steal, even if only a few dollars. Take the time to develop and train all volunteers and employees about cash-handling policies and procedures.

Following are some general guidelines and things to think about that can help you develop a cash-handling policy specific to your church.

Example: Cash-Handling Policy

Cash-Handling Policy
Purpose: To ensure control and safekeeping of church donations and cash assets and to minimize the risk of embezzlement.

• Use a safe to store all cash. Even small amounts of cash (petty cash), and secure cash register drawers under lock and key at all times.
• Have two unrelated people count the weekly offering.
• Rotate counting volunteers; have a lead volunteer or church employee supervise them.
• Have two people present whenever transporting cash from one location to another.
• Keep a cash count sheet that documents:
    o Names of people counting, depositing, or removing cash from safe
    o Date/time cash is deposited or removed from safe
    o Date/time cash is removed or returned to safe
    o Cash breakdown—coins, bills, checks, credit card slips
    o Two signature lines for people handling cash
• Only open safes with two people present.
• The person with the combination to the safe should not be one of the people involved in handling the cash in the safe.
• The person with the combination to the safe should not have a key or access to the room where the safe is kept.
• When removing cash bags from the safe, two people should count it, and both people should sign the cash count sheet acknowledging that the recorded amount of cash was in the bag.
• When these people hand off the cash to the next person, the person accepting the cash should count the cash before accepting it and keep the signed copy of the cash record with the cash.
• When the next two people return cash to the safe, double count it and both people must sign the cash count sheet.
• Bank deposit slips should match the cash-handling sheets.
• Keep all records on all cash deposits.

These are very simple guidelines and can expand and adapt to your particular church.

Other things to think about:

- Where is the safe located?
- Is the safe out of public sight?
- Who has keys to the room the safe is in? The person who has keys to the room should not be the same person who has the combination to the safe.
- Always conduct background checks on employees and volunteers who handle cash. Some organizations do credit checks to find out whether there are financial issues with employees.
- Change safe combinations whenever a person holding the combination leaves employment.
- A drop slot in the safe allows for one-way access to the safe, eliminating the need to unlock the safe every time someone deposits a cash bag in the safe.
- Another must is a camera to monitor all safes and cash registers, particularly those that are isolated and out of a manager's sight.

Organizations lose billions of dollars each year from embezzlement, and churches are not exempt. Safeguarding against embezzlement in the church is a leadership responsibility. Good policies, procedures, and oversight of cash handling are ways to safeguard against theft of church cash.

What does your church do to prevent embezzlement of church funds?

Responsible Stewardship

God blesses churches with many resources, people, time, and money, and He expects us to be good stewards with what He provides.

Members tithe on their income to support the operation of the ministry, making it even more important to be good stewards and manage financial resources responsibly.

So what is the definition of stewardship?

Stewardship is "the responsible overseeing and protection of something considered worth caring for and preserving."

In the church, stewardship is the responsible oversight of church funds, property, and equipment.

5 Keys to Responsible Church Stewardship

1. Know What You're Trying to Accomplish

Responsible Stewardship

The first important step to good stewardship knows why you exist and what you're trying to accomplish. The church does this by creating a mission that articulates its purpose and what it hopes to achieve as an organization. This important first step sets the direction and decision-making model for the ministry.

2. Budget Toward the Vision

The next step is to create an annual budget that funds the vision. This includes looking at those strategic objectives that require financial support and allocating dollars to support those church goals.

For example, if the vision results in a strategy that includes outreach to the poor, allocate dollars for the development of an outreach program. This may include funding for administrative oversight, supplies, and marketing materials.

3. Wise Spending Decisions

The church makes spending decisions as it allocates dollars to fund its different strategies, and using wisdom in that spending is critical to good stewardship. A decision model that helps with prioritizing spending is asking the question, is this something we want, need, or have-to-have.

In other words, is this something we would like (want), something that would help us do our job better (need) or is this something that is mission critical to fulfill strategy (have-to-have). For example, developing an outreach program may require purchasing equipment and a decision may be made to purchase a new or used piece of equipment.

The goal is to get the best value for the dollar without sacrificing quality. It does the church no benefit to buy a used computer that lasts only a year when spending a few more dollars will ensure the computer is around for several years.

4. Accountability for Managing Funds

A church budget guides spending decisions, but it's also important to make sure that those budgeted dollars are spent on those things that it was allocated for.

A budget review process ensures that monthly spending does not exceed the monthly-allocated dollars. A budget review or finance committee would be the right group to do this.

If there are variances in the budget, address and reconcile them on a monthly basis. This helps to ensure there are no surprises at the end of the year.

5. Conflict of Interest

Always make decisions on spending ministry resources with the best interest of the organization in mind. This means ensuring the responsible people make comparisons on large purchases or when securing vendor relationships. Allowing family, friends, and members to bid is okay as long as vendor decisions are in the best interest of the church, not the friend.

A good rule of thumb is to get three bids and choose the vendor with the best quality for the price. Cheapest isn't always better if the product or service is inferior.

Every organization should be good stewards with the resources they have, but the church needs to meet an even higher standard since the resources they're provided come from the sacrifice of their members. The church can never lose sight of the fact that this is God's money.

Code of Conduct

"The most important persuasion tool you have in your entire arsenal is integrity."
Zig Ziglar

An organization builds its reputation on the consistency of ethical behavior its leaders and employees demonstrate.

For a church, this reputation is what attracts and retains members, volunteers, and employees.

Many organizations create code of ethics and conduct statements as a way to communicate established boundaries and set expectations for employee behavior. This document also serves as a tool to self-regulate and helps to guide decision-making.

This code includes things like conflicts of interest, confidentiality, respect for each other, legal compliance, etc. The church board is responsible for determining the boundaries for ethical behavior.

Don't be naive enough to think that church employees are exempt from unethical conduct. Having a written code of conduct that employees sign when hired helps employees understand ethical behavior expectations.

Some examples of what can go in a code of conduct:

Management Practices

Management practices are the underlying foundation for organizational integrity, whether it's a commitment to serving the members or managing employment practices. Unresolved issues can tarnish a ministry's reputation, and employees observe how leadership responds to issues and follows up on promises made. Employees who trust management are more engaged and supportive of ministry efforts.

How Leaders Communicate

Good communication is critical to the success of any organization but specifically to organizations built on their members' trust and donations. People involved in a ministry have an interest in what the organization does and how they're performing. Sharing information is a way to keep members informed and engaged. Church leaders and employees should take measures to actively communicate any information that would benefit others and improve the church or work experience.

Food for thought: Do you hoard information that you should share with others because it makes you feel empowered?

Be a Good Steward of God's Resources

God supplies church resources—people, time, and money. Church leaders and employees must remember to serve as good stewards of those resources.They must exercise good time management skills, create an annual operating budget, and hold leadership accountable for adhering to spending guidelines.

Food for thought: Do you spend church resources only on those things that support its mission?

Treat Everyone with Dignity and Respect

Employees should respect everyone in the body of Christ and treat everyone the same, regardless of rank or socioeconomic position.

Food for thought: Do the big givers in your church get preferential treatment?

Streamlined Processes

Church staff should continually look for ways to improve those processes and systems that affect the church experience for volunteers, members, and employees.

Food for thought: Do you take the time to consider how internal processes affect your key customers—members, volunteers, and employees?

Compliance with Policy

Church employees must comply with all policies as set forth by the ministry.

Food for thought: Do all employees comply with all church policies?

Confidentiality

Church employees should maintain the highest standard of confidentiality and share sensitive information only with those who have a need to know. This includes information about the internal operations of the church as well as information about church members and volunteers.

Food for thought: Do you discuss personal issues (gossip) about members with others who have no need to know?

Comply With Legal Requirements

The day-to-day operation of the church needs to comply with all governing laws and regulations. Writing policies and procedures to ensure legal compliance achieves this. Perform annual audits to ensure consistency in practice and compliance with regulations.

Food for thought: Are there questionable internal practices that you worry others will uncover and challenge?

Conflict of Interest

Church leaders and employees have a duty to act in the best interest of the church at all times. What this means is there's a duty of loyalty that supersedes anything that could result in personal gain by avoiding conflicts of interest or anything that may appear to be a conflict.

Food for thought: Do you conduct church business with vendors you have a personal financial interest in?

These are just some examples of things that could go in a church code of ethics and conduct statement. Acknowledge employees who demonstrate desired behaviors and confront and correct employees who do not. The church board typically develops code of ethics and conduct statements, and then they filter them throughout the organization through training and the orientation process.

Depending on the industry, code of ethics and conduct statements are of varying lengths. The more an industry is regulated (for instance, financial services) the more in-depth the statements become. The key is to develop a document that reflects the desired integrity of the organization, in a format that employees can interpret and understand.

Organizations define desired behaviors and use driving principles to guide decision-making. The actions of church leaders reflect the organizations' desired behavior and values.

Additionally, the behavior that employees observe in leaders is what they learn is acceptable. Leadership needs to walk the talk to reinforce this behavior. Setting desired behavior expectations, and holding employees accountable, is the first step in creating a culture that fosters high standards of ethical conduct.

Managing Communication

Managing communication is critical to the success of any organization, but specifically nonprofits that build themselves on the trust and donations of their members. People involved in a ministry have an interest in what the organization does and how they are performing within it.

Church communication management is about sharing information in a way that keeps members informed and engaged. Being proactive requires having a process for communicating information that members and donors have an interest in.

Tips for Managing Church Communications

Create a Process for Communicating

The process of communication is important because it sets the expectation for how to share information. Structure this process enough so that those receiving the communication can reasonably predict how and when they will receive it. For example, a new volunteer may receive information about his/her job assignment in a number of ways: via email, postal letter, telephone, or church website. Regardless of how he/she receives the assignment, include a defined communication process for receiving the information.

Another example might be how church members receive information about new projects the church is working on. Things like adding space to the facilities, creating new staff positions, or a new program under development are all things members are interested in.

Interested parties may receive this kind of information at church meetings, by pulpit announcements, in postal letters, or on the church website. The communication process is not as important as its consistency and thoroughness. The secret to effective communication is to answer the questions before they're asked!

Determine What Gets Communicated

Church congregants, volunteers, and employees need to receive lots of information, and they should have a good understanding of what kinds of information they can expect. The ministry should have defined guidelines for what it communicates, to whom, how often, and in what format. For example, you should determine whether it's standard practice to share information about major church purchases or initiatives during the planning phase, budgeting phase, or after all the details are complete?

Regardless, church communications should adhere to pre-established guidelines used to steer information sharing. Guidelines should specify what kind of information is shared, the process for sharing the information, and the timeliness of what is communicated.

Consistency in communication helps gain trust and credibility with those whom the church serves.

Identifying a communication advocate is the best way to ensure effective information sharing. This person is responsible for thinking about **who** needs to know what information, **when** to share the information, and **how** to share the information.

Incorporate Two-way Communication

Two-way communication is important because it helps to minimize misunderstandings, and it helps to engage others. When people can ask clarifying questions, it helps to resolve issues, and it opens the door for better understanding and buy-in.

This kind of communication can take place on a one-on-one basis, in large group open-forum settings, member focus groups or electronically via the website or other feedback tools. It's important to develop processes to encourage two-way communication with the congregation, volunteers, and employees.

Leadership is all about the process of leading others. This includes how to share information, how well others receive the communication, and how well the leadership keeps the mission and vision in front of the people.

Leadership is all about the "process" of leading others. This includes how leaders share information, how well they communicate with others, and how well they keep the vision in front of the people.

CHAPTER 5

Problem-Solving and Decision-Making

"Let us not become weary in doing good, for at the proper time we will reap a harvest if we do not give up."
Galatians 6:9

Problem-Solving and Decision-Making

Managing church operations presents many challenges and calls for daily decisions. Decisions need to have a structured process to ensure that all decisions are consistent, unbiased, and principled. The responsibility of church leadership is to implement a strategy and accomplish goals. For example, in the game of football, there's a lot of strategy and effort that goes into the game, but at the end of the day, scoring touchdowns is all that matters.

Similarly, with leadership, accomplishing goals is its responsibility, and the way it manages the team determines how well the team accomplishes goals and how well the leadership allows the team to get the ball into the end zone.

Use the Vision as the Guide

The beauty of developing a mission, vision, and values statement is that it provides the framework for decision-making.

All high-level decisions should filter through the mission and vision, and have this question answered, "Does this line up with our mission, vision, and values?"

The second question is, "Do we have or can we solicit the resources needed for this?"

Eliminate Bottlenecks

Decisions often stop at a bottleneck in the hierarchy and the decision-making process. This happens when decisions that someone needs to make is stuck at a decision point. This is typically a decision that only one person can make and the hesitation in making that decision holds up the entire process.

Here's an example. The decision is to paint the office's interior walls. The painting team is ready to go, but is waiting on the decision regarding the paint colors. The goal is to paint the offices before the office open house in January, but the team assigned to paint is waiting for someone to pick the colors.

In this example, the person who is responsible for choosing the color delayed making the decision, which resulted in the team not being able to achieve the goal. A solution to this example would be for the facility review council to create a palate of approved colors and then empower the painting team to choose one of those colors. This is an example of creating systems and procedures to speed up the process and empower employees to make decisions that help achieve objectives.

Difficult Decisions

Making difficult decisions is inevitable, and sometimes those decisions are painful because they affect the lives of others. It may be a decision to end the relationship with a vendor who isn't delivering what was promised. Perhaps, this vendor just happens to be a church member or an employee who isn't fulfilling her job responsibilities and needs to be terminated, but her entire extended family attends the church.

Perhaps a longtime volunteer has been caught doing an illegal activity and needs to be asked to step down from a key leadership position.

Regardless, these kinds of issues come up in church life, and leadership needs to address the issues and make the tough decisions. Sometimes difficult decisions have an impact on the entire church, and the way church leaders make and communicate the decision can have a global effect.

For example, if the church is experiencing rapid growth and it needs new leadership to take the church to the next level, someone has to make the difficult decision of changing leadership. Acting on that decision quickly or slowly can have an impact on those affected by that decision.

When faced with these kinds of decisions, I always ask this question: "Do you like to take a Band-Aid off slowly or quickly?"

Acting on a decision quickly can create a lot of sudden pain, but you can adjust to the pain quickly, and it will go away.

Another approach is to take the Band-Aid off slowly. This approach takes a little more time, is less painful, and adjustment is slower, but it's still painful.

Each approach has its advantages and disadvantages. The question is what's the best approach for any particular situation?

> "To let people languish in uncertainty for months or years…when in the end they aren't going to make it anyway—that would be *ruthless*. To deal with it right up front and let people get on with their lives—that is *rigorous*." Jim Collins, Good to Great

Problem-Solving Tools

Problems. It sometimes seems as if we solve one problem and another one pops up right behind it. Why? Because fixing a problem creates new problems! Think about these examples:

Scenario Problem: A church of 1000 members creates strategies and sets goals to increase membership by 50%.

They are successful with their endeavors and now they have a new problem: not enough seating for the new members and not enough children's ministry space for the increased number of kids.

New problem: We need more space.

The team puts together a recommendation to add another service to take the stress off of one weekly service. A second service begins. Problem solved.

New problem: We need more volunteers for the second service.

As you can see, those who manage any type of organization have to solve problems. The tools they use can vary from gut instincts to structured problem-solving tools. Skilled managers are good problem-solvers and use problem-solving tools to help them find the best solutions.

"You have to be smarter than the problem." John Stiffler

Any organization that's growing is constantly solving one problem that creates a new problem. Having problems to solve is not necessarily a bad thing, but the solutions are best when they're part of an established problem-solving process.

The secret is having a structured problem-solving process; this is total quality management. Quality concepts provide problem-solving tools that can help identify problems and provide ways to solve problems.

> "Quality is never an accident; it is always the result of high intention, sincere effort, intelligent direction and skillful execution; it represents the wise choice of many alternatives." Attributed to William Foster

Organizations use quality tools to solve problems and monitor and manage improvement initiatives. There are several types of tools used, but here we'll talk about the most common ones. There are different tools for solving different problems, and many different uses for these tools. The trick is to become familiar with and comfortable with all the quality management tools so you can pull the appropriate one out of your toolbox when there's a problem to solve.

5 Whys

One quality problem-solving tool is the "5 Whys." This exercise can quickly get to the root of a problem. It's tempting to jump to the first conclusion when trying to solve a problem so it's important to make sure that what's thought to be the root of the problem truly is. Let's look at this example.

Problem: The children's ministry has to turn away children because there aren't enough workers to comply with teacher-to-student ratios.

Let's look at this problem and ask the question why five times.

Why? The first answer might be that all of the scheduled workers don't always show up for their shifts.

Why? When calling the workers who didn't show up for their shifts, a few answered, "I didn't know I was scheduled."

Why? Workers didn't receive their monthly schedule in the mail.

Why? Workers were on the mailing list, and their schedules were mailed, but they didn't receive the mail.

Why? Workers moved but didn't notify the office of address changes.

Now if you look at the answer to the first "why" and stop there, you may have the tendency to lay blame on the workers and jump to the conclusion that these workers are irresponsible and unreliable. But as you ask why for the fourth and fifth time, you'll see a clearer picture of the issue.

Here's one of my favorite quality quotes, "It's not about the people; it's about the process." If you put good people in bad processes, the outcomes don't improve.

When problems arise, it's human nature to try to find the culprit and lay blame on someone, but more times than not, the person is working in a broken process that limits his or her ability to perform well.

Let's look at another example. Imagine that you have a receptionist and you're constantly getting complaints that she doesn't know the answers to callers' questions, and she continues to transfer callers to the wrong person or wrong department. You can discipline that employee or you can try to learn what in the process isn't working. Going through the five whys could flush out reasons and possible solutions. Let's look at this example.

Problem: Complaints about receptionist.

Why? The receptionist doesn't know answers to questions or gives out wrong information.

Why? The receptionist manual doesn't have accurate answers to common questions.

Why? No one updated the receptionist manual, as scheduled.

Why? No one gave changing information to the receptionist to update the manual.

Why? The administrative assistant who takes minutes at manager's meeting doesn't pass information along to the receptionist.

Why? No one told the administrative assistant to pass the info along during her job review.

As you can see from this example, the problem is a training issue but not with the receptionist. We couldn't have identified the problem without asking the question at least five times. These examples demonstrate that once you separate the person from the problem, you can find the causes and fix the process that will, ultimately, fix the person. Employees come to work and want to do a good job. In order for that to happen, those who manage them are responsible to make sure the work processes make sense and help the employee do a good job.

Following are the seven most common quality tools. Each has an example for use in solving church problems.

Flowchart

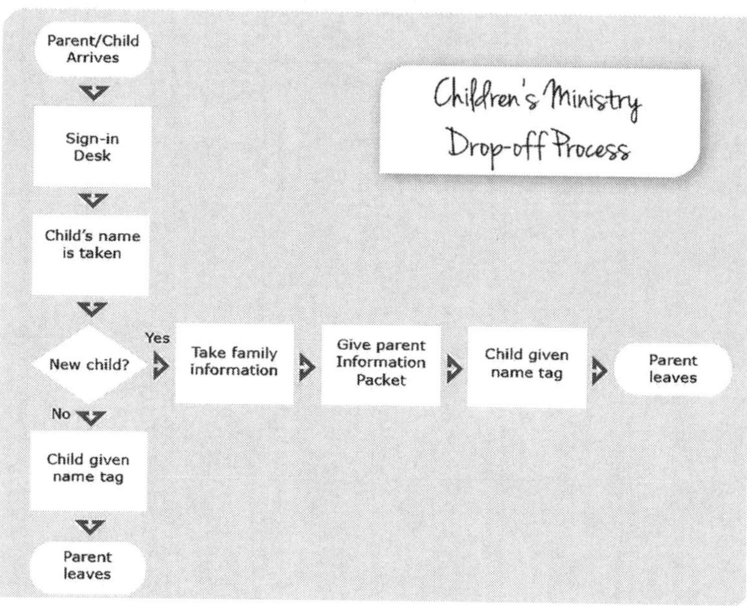

Most of us are familiar with flowcharts. You have seen flowcharts of reporting relationships in organizational structures. Flowcharts also help to document process flows. Use this tool when trying to figure out bottlenecks or breakdowns in current processes.

Flowcharting the steps of a process gives a picture of what the process looks like and can shed light on issues within the process. Flowcharts also show changes in processes to show improvements or a new workflow process.

Check Sheet

Check Sheet		
Date: May 10, 20XX		
Problem: Volunteer not showing up as scheduled		
Reason	Number of Volunteers	Subtotal
Did not receive schedule	///// ///// /////	15
Forgot	///// ///	8
Sick/Family Emergency	///// ///// ///// //	17
Issue with volunteer role	///// ///	8
Other	///// //	7
	Grand Total	55

A check sheet is a basic quality tool used to collect data. A check sheet might track the number of times a certain incident happens. As an example, a large church that schedules hundreds of volunteers to serve at every church service may track the number of times volunteers don't show up for scheduled shifts. This check sheet would total the number of times a volunteer doesn't report as scheduled compared to the reasons for the volunteer not showing up. This data paints a picture for what is influencing why volunteers don't show up for scheduled shifts.

Cause and Effect Diagram

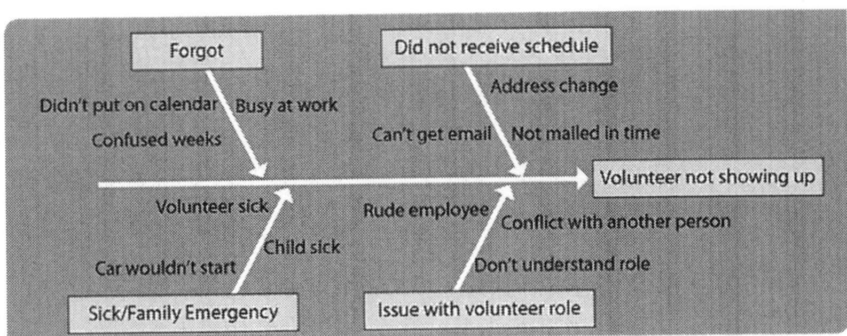

A cause and effect diagram, also known as a fishbone diagram, shows a problem's different causes. Identify and write the problem in the box (head of the fish) to the right. There's then a spine of the fish, and then off the spine are major causes of the problem. Causes typically go into categories of people, processes, materials, and equipment. Brainstorming with a group familiar with the problem identifies causes. Once identified, the group can develop an improvement plan to help resolve the problem.

Pareto Chart

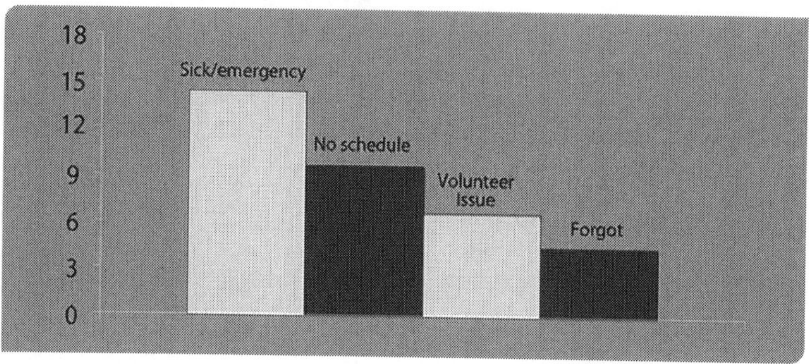

A Pareto chart is a bar graph of data showing the largest number of frequencies to the smallest. When looked at from largest to the smallest occurrences, it's an easy picture to see how to prioritize improvement efforts. The most significant problems stand out and can be the first target.

In this example, there's not much you can do about volunteer emergencies. But, if you can fix the schedule problem, and work on eliminating other volunteer issues, you can reduce the number of volunteers not showing up.

Control Charts

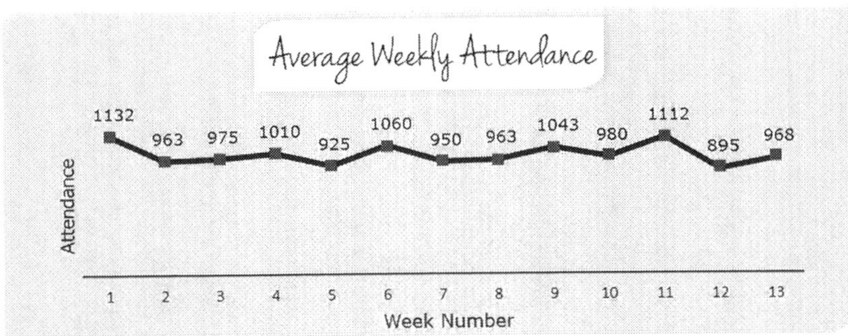

Control charts or run charts plot data points on a line over time and give a picture of data movement. It demonstrates when data is consistent or when there are high or low outliers in occurrences of data. It focuses on monitoring performance over time by looking at variations in data points. It distinguishes between common cause and special cause variations. The Dow Jones Industrial Average is a good example of a control chart.

Churches use control charts to look for attendance and giving trends. For example, there are natural spikes in attendance on Easter and Christmas.

Histograms

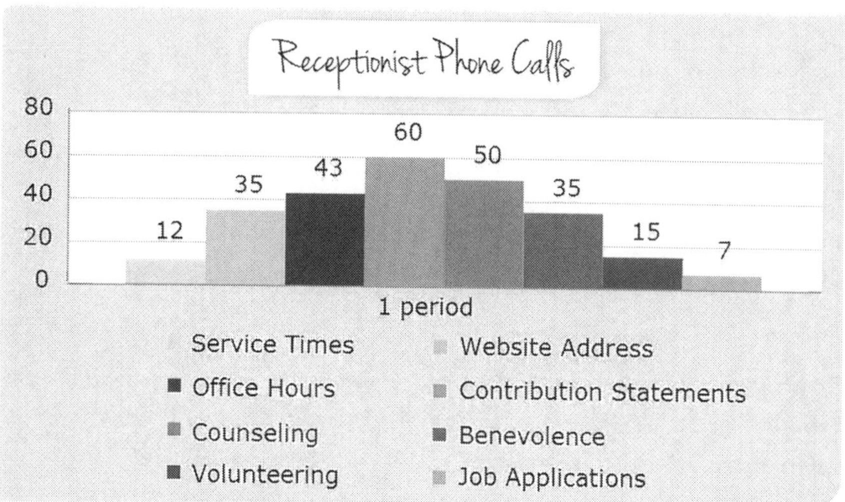

A histogram is a bar chart picture that shows patterns in data that fall within typical process conditions. Changes in a process should trigger new collection of data. For example, the histogram above shows the highest volumes of phone calls are to ask about contribution statements. This is a seasonal high number that should redistribute over time. Gather a minimum of 50 to 75 data points to ensure an adequate number of data points.

This could mean collecting data on phone calls over several weeks or even months. The detected patterns demonstrate an analysis that helps understand variation and provides information to use to improve an internal communication process.

Scatter diagrams

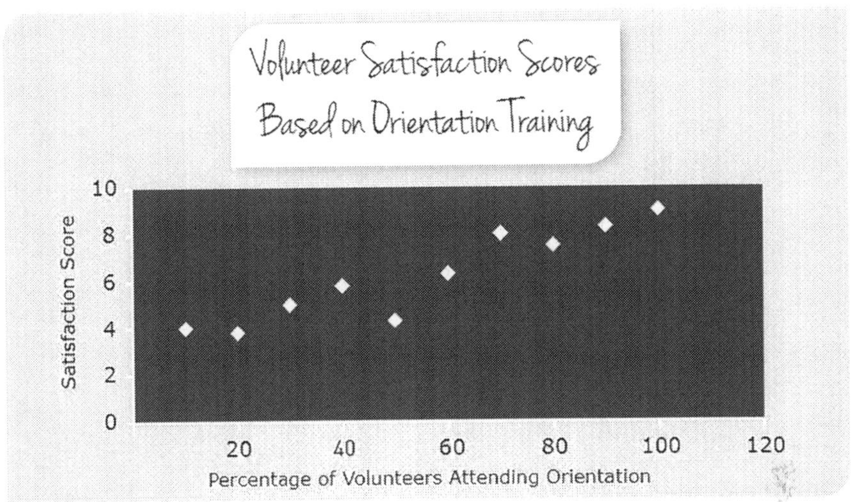

Scatter diagrams are graphs that show the relationship between variables. Variables often represent possible causes and effect. As an example, a scatter might show how volunteer training affects volunteer satisfaction scores. This diagram shows the relationship between the percentage of volunteers going through a formal orientation process and volunteer satisfaction scores.

Each tool has advantages for certain situations, but not all tools are for all problem solving. Once people learn a tool, they can adapt it to different problem-solving opportunities. As with anything else, using tools properly takes time, practice, and experience.

How Can FOCUS PDCA Help Improve Church Operations?

Improving what we do and how we do it is an important part of operational strategy. As churches develop and grow, improvement opportunities will present themselves along the way. Opportunities can arise in business processes like the accounting function, a children's ministry check-in process, or a volunteer orientation process aimed to improve the congregant experience. No matter what the process is, there probably is a systematic approach to making improvements.

A quality method for improving work processes is a model called FOCUS PDCA. This methodology takes a process through identification of the improvement opportunity, planning for an improvement, and implementation and evaluation of the change.

The first step in any improvement is to understand the current process by establishing a baseline. A baseline is measurable data that's collected at the beginning of an improvement project. For example, if you want to improve the length of the volunteer application process, it's important to measure what the current application process time is.

Once you know what the current process time is, you can identify those things that slow the process down and then develop systems to improve those times. Conduct measurement of any improvement effort at the beginning, during, and after any improvement effort.

So how does FOCUS PDCA Work?

FOCUS PDCA is an acronym for:

Find: An opportunity for improvement.

Organize: A team that's familiar with the process.

Clarify: Understand the process.

Understand: Variations in the process.

Select: What needs improvement.

Plan: Develop an improvement plan.

Do: Execute the plan.

Check: Review the results and determine whether the plan worked.

Act: If the plan worked, standardize the change and write policy. If the plan did not work, go back and try something else.

Let's look at an example of how this might work. Say you're a church that processes dozens of volunteer applications every month. You've noticed an increasing numbers of complaints about the length of time it takes to process, approve, and place volunteers. The church is growing, but you're concerned that the complaints will have an impact on future volunteer interest. Let's use this example and go through the cycle.

FOCUS PDCA Cycle:

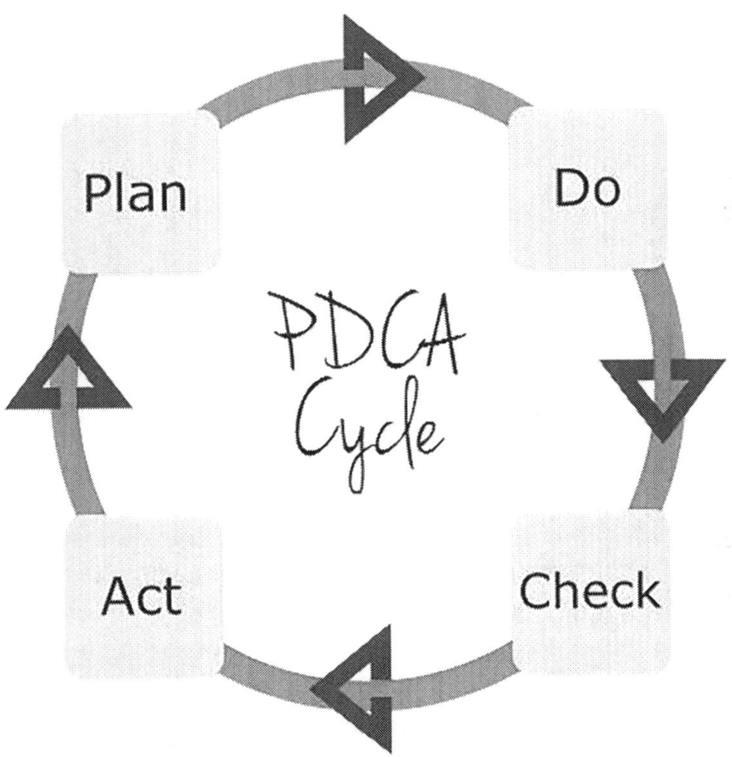

Find: The opportunity to improve is in the volunteer application process.

Organize: Recruit a team of employees who oversee volunteers and manage the volunteer application process.

Clarify: Map out the volunteer application process in a flowchart. Start with the point at which you receive the application and map the process through volunteer placement.

Understand: Collect data so you understand any variations in the process.

Select: Identify what in the process can be improved.

Plan: Develop an improvement plan.

Do: Implement the plan.

Check: Collect data to see how the plan worked.

Act: If the plan worked, write a policy and train employees on the new process. If the plan didn't work, go back to the beginning and try another improvement idea.

This is a very simplified example of using FOCUS PDCA, but what you will find is that if you try this method on a few small improvement opportunities, you will become more comfortable and can use the same methodology on larger system problems.

Guiding Councils

In Jim Collins' book, Good to Great, he talks about using councils to help guide the organization. Councils should have a group of the right people to discuss, debate, and make decisions about the organization's operation.

People selected to serve on councils should be those with knowledge, experience, and a passion for the topic. The board should steer these knowledge experts and use them to facilitate a decision-making process that benefits the church.

Councils should have a charter, and someone must facilitate the process. This facilitator should help the council identify a team, create a team charter, determine ground rules, and create team goals. By going through this process, the team has some accountability and a set direction. Councils should meet regularly and report to the church board.

Examples of Church Councils

Budget Review

The budget review council should meet monthly to review monthly budget numbers, analyze budget variances, and approve non-budget expenditures. This group is also responsible for meeting with church managers and creating the annual budget.

The budgeting process forecasts annual revenues, notates fixed and flexible spending, and anticipates and budgets for large capital expenses. This group is the financial think-tank and has an identified representative that reports to the board of directors.

Human Resource Council

The human resource council helps to ensure that policies, procedures, and processes are in place to support staff and volunteers, and that the ministry complies with and operates within state and federal laws. An HR council might also have responsibility to review job applications and approve applicants for the first round of interviews.

The HR Council should also help to establish employee pay grades, make decisions on employee benefits, employee policies, training, tuition reimbursement, leadership development, job classifications, employee assistance programs, vacation approval process, reward and recognition, and performance management.

Facility Review Council

The facility review council should meet on a regular basis and discuss strategy for maintaining the current facility, identifying facility update needs, and plan for future expansions or remodels. This group also facilitates the process of ensuring that staff work areas meet employee job requirements and gives direction on standard furniture, décor colors, campus directions, and mechanical equipment needs. This council meets with the budget review committee to budget large capital expenditures and ensure resources are available when needed.

Information Technology

The information technology council is responsible for making sure the church has the necessary technology to run its operations. This may include recommending purchases of audiovisual equipment for church services and computer software to operate the children's ministry or assessing whether employees have the right computer equipment and software to perform their job duties.

This council also researches new technologies and ensures the church uses all available technologies that facilitate streamlined work processes. For example, investing in electronic scanning systems for the children's ministry and adult classes can eliminate the need to manually input attendance information into the church database.

This council is also responsible for establishing ministry guidelines for replacing computers, setting guidelines for Internet usage, training employees in proper email etiquette, communicating policies on employee personal use of church equipment, and establishing any other information technology parameters.

Safety Council

A safety council is responsible for ensuring the church provides a safe environment for visitors and employees. The council does this by reviewing safety procedures for potentially dangerous activities by employees and volunteers.

This group should make routine campus rounds and actively look for hazards that need correcting.

This could be anything within buildings or outside grounds, things like electrical systems, walking surfaces, air quality, fire extinguishers, clutter in hallways, etc. Making a point of looking for things that could pose a threat of harm to employees or visitors can help to avoid an unnecessary incident of injury.

Customer Experience Council

A customer experience council is responsible for seeking feedback from all customer groups—congregant, volunteers, and employees—and identifying ways to improve the experience. This council may be responsible for facilitating a formal feedback process, reviewing feedback data, and developing improvement plans based on that data. For example, this group may find that volunteers are asking for a more structured training process because they don't feel adequately trained to perform their job duties.

Guiding councils may charter teams to help improve their systems and process and work on improvement efforts. Organizational directives and a team charter steer successful teams.

According to **www.highperformanceteams.org**, a team charter statement is "a written document that defines the team's mission, scope of operation, objectives, time frame and consequences."Spending the time to develop a team charter and purpose statement can help ensure team support and resource availability. A charter helps clarify support and resource allocation from management. This formal document legitimizes the team's efforts and supports the team so they can accomplish their tasks.

A team charter document should include:

Purpose Statement

The purpose statement explains why a team exists and how its charge lines up with the global goals of the organization. For example,

"The purpose of the Customer Experience Council is to improve customer satisfaction scores for Regional Community Church."

Mission Statement

A mission statement clarifies the team's responsibility. For example, "The mission of the Budget Review Council is to ensure proper management and control of church financial resources."

Scope of Operation

The scope of the operation details the boundaries and parameters the team operates within. For example, "The Human Resource Council will research and make recommendations on hiring, firing, and compensation and benefits for church employees according to best practice benchmarks and within legal and tax compliance."

Team Objectives

Tie the objectives of a team to measurable results. These objectives should demonstrate the effectiveness of the team. For example, "The Budget Review Council will control church expenditures and maintain a 5 percent profit margin."

Time Frame

Clearly define the time frame for any team project so the team understands the deadlines and urgency for completing its commission. For example, "The Facility Review Council will ensure all church facilities are maintained with appropriate updates on an annual basis."

Consequences

Chartered teams use organization resources, and the team is accountable for producing the results outlined in the team charter.

The accountability outlined in the document must be specific so that members understand the importance of their commitment to the council. It's important for newly chartered councils to understand why the group exists, what their charge is, the time frame in which they need to accomplish the tasks and accountability for meeting team objectives. This very clear communication and process on the front end of a team launch can help prevent miscommunication issues.

CHAPTER 6

Managing the Money

"Shepherd the flock of God which is among you, serving as overseers, not by compulsion but willingly, not for dishonest gain but eagerly; nor as being lords over those entrusted to you, but being examples to the flock;"
1 Peter 5:2-3

Budgeting

God blesses churches with tithing members to provide the resources to do the ministry's work. Good stewardship of those resources is a serious responsibility.

Churches that use an operating budget have to control spending, and budgeting toward the vision should always be the goal. Formalizing the budgeting process can help ensure that dollars go to those things that help move the organization forward. It's surprising, but many organizations don't operate with a budget because they question the value of taking the time to prepare and monitor the budget.

Reasons to Budget

✓ Achieving objectives is no accident; it takes a plan supported by budget dollars to achieve.

- ✓ The budgeting process forces organizational planning and goal setting and creates a structured process for funding church-wide initiatives and objectives.
- ✓ Budgeted goals and objectives are useful as tools to evaluate performance.
- ✓ Budgeting helps to facilitate strategic plan implementation by allocating resources to strategic priorities.
- ✓ Budgeting eliminates turf wars over spending and available resources.
- ✓ Budgeting improves communication throughout the organization because everyone understands what the priorities and resources are for each department.

Budgets are for both planning and control. **Planning** requires high-level decisions about priorities that line up with strategy, while **controlling** ensures that management implements the plan and achieves objectives. Planning is futile without control over spending, and without planning, there are no targeted objectives to achieve.

Budgets set targets for revenues and spending and establish a plan for how the church will achieve its short and long-term strategies. The budgeting process makes estimates of revenues, plans expenditures, and restricts spending that isn't part of the plan.

Operating budgets extend out for one year and divide into four quarters. The quarters then divide into months, and the financial people view the budget on a monthly basis to review gains, losses, and variances.

The manager's supervisor bases the manager performance on how well he or she handles the department budget and holds the manager accountable for variances between the budget and actual results. Different levels of management organize and control budget costs. Historical performance and strategic priorities form the basis for budget allocation.

Having a formal and structured budgeting process is the foundation for good stewardship. Very similar to our personal finances, discipline and planning are cornerstones of a church budgeting process.

As with most things in managing a church, the organization's vision and the strategic plan drive budgeting needs. Churches that stay focused on their strategy and plan know exactly where they want to spend their resources and have a plan to help keep them from spending in areas that don't line up with the vision.

For example, does spending $100,000 on a new sound system for the church auditorium line up with church strategy? How would your church answer this question?

The Budgeting Process

The budget review committee establishes the global budget with revenue projections and allocates dollars to individual departments. The individual department managers are responsible for creating their own budget estimates based on goals and allocated resources.

Allowing individual department managers to prepare their own budget estimates makes them more accountable, accurate, and reliable. The advantage to this approach is working managers are more apt to follow their own budgets because they created the budget and understand the reasoning behind it as opposed to a budget handed down to them from above. This adds a layer of accountability in that the manager has no one else to blame for failing to meet their own budget requirements.

Top management sets strategy and goals, and then managers and supervisors estimate budget requirements needed to accomplish the strategy. Once prepared, the managers submit their budgets to the next level of management for review and approval. Then the negotiations start until a final budget gets approval.

Department managers often get caught in the middle, and many express these common concerns with budgets:

- ✓ If I don't spend all the budgeted dollars this year, will I lose that money next year? For example, facilities has $10,000 budgeted for snow removal but used only $7,500 because of a mild winter. Should facilities receive $10,000 for the budget next year?
- ✓ If I overspend my budget, will it reflect on my performance appraisal? For example, a severe winter caused the snow removal budget to go above the $10,000 to $15,000. Is the facilities manager responsible for this variance?
- ✓ I don't want budget restraints to affect employees, congregants, or improvement efforts. For example, if the scanning system for the children's ministry check-in breaks and there are no dollars in the budget to replace it, what happens to the employees' and parents' experience? Is this an acceptable variance?
- ✓ If there's too much focus on budget control, it can take the focus off nonfinancial goals and targets. For example, if the children's ministry manager is more concerned with controlling spending than making sure her department meets the needs of the parents (customers), the priority to have positive responses from parents may be challenged. There needs to be a balance.

Strategic Plan

Having a well thought-out strategic plan that supports the church vision is the first step in any budgeting process. Use church resources to implement strategy and develop the ministry, and budgeted dollars make it happen.

Church Goals

Developing goals is the next step in the budgeting process. A well-thought-out strategic plan generates annual church goals that the budget needs to fund. Accountability for achieving goals is the responsibility of the church board or governing body.

Revenue Projections

Historical financial performance and projected church growth income are the basis for revenue projections. The projected growth can tie into organizational goals and planned initiatives that will initiate financial growth. For example, if a goal is to increase contributions by 10 percent, those contribution projections should be part of the revenue forecast for the year.

Additionally, if the economic downturn still affects your congregation, it may be wise to be conservative with projections. The last thing a church needs is to fall short of a forecast and not meet budget requirements.

Fixed Cost Projections

Projecting fixed costs is simply a matter of looking at the monthly predictable costs that do not change, things like employee compensation costs, mortgage or rent payments, insurance costs, etc. Fixed costs do not change and are minimum monthly expenses that need a line in the budget. For example, if there are open staff positions, the cost to fill those positions is a fixed cost projection. Fixed costs are the most controllable and predictable expenses, but they need management and consistent review for cost-saving opportunities.

Variable Cost Projections

Variable costs are the expenses that fluctuate from month to month. Things like supply costs, travel, utilities, and overtime operating expenses are all examples of variable expenses.

These expenses can be budgeted and controlled, but sometimes things happen that are beyond anyone's control. An example of this is snow removal costs in an extreme winter when the normal cost doubles.

A good way to control variable costs is to put monthly limits on things like travel and supply costs or overtime and to hold managers accountable to stay within the set limits.

Annual Goal Expenses

Any project or program that's part of an outlined strategy should also have a budget. Each initiative should have projected costs associated with the goals and be managed like any other budget line item. This is where the cost of implementing goals incorporates into the annual budget. Identify projections of costs, lay them out and incorporate them into the departmental budget that's responsible for that goal. For example, if the church is strategically targeting young families, there may be a goal to develop a young married couple's ministry. This would require funding to plan, staff, and market the initiative, and this requires budget dollars.

Target Profit Margin

Every organization, whether it's a for-profit or not-for-profit, should have a targeted profit margin. Not-for-profit organizations use profit margins to reinvest into the facilities and the organization's development.

Profits are important for all organizations. Healthy profit margins are a strong indicator of the strength of an organization and help fund new programs and facilities. A profit margin also acts as a buffer if revenue projections fall short.

Board Approval

The governing board should approve the budget and monitor budget performance. The budget review committee is responsible for reviewing monthly financial statements to monitor budget performance, become familiar with all expenditures, and safeguard the organization against misappropriation of funds. It's counter-intuitive to think there could be fraudulent activity in a church setting, but don't be naive to the possibility. The more people there are to oversee and challenge the budgeting process, the stronger the bottom line becomes.

Budget Review

The budget review council should meet monthly to monitor performance against goals, review budget variances, and assess issues associated with budget variances. It's important to do this every month so there can be a correction to overspending or a modification to the budget, if needed. This includes monitoring revenue projections when compared with cost. Waiting until the end of the year to make corrections could negatively affect the final budget outcome.

How to Deal With Budget Variances

Review variances with the responsible department manager and raise questions about what caused the variance. Sometimes unforeseen situations arise that are unavoidable, so it's important to have a budgeted emergency fund to help with those unplanned expenditures.

For example, if the HVAC system suddenly goes down and needs replacement, this is a justified budget variance. However, a manager's overspending on unnecessary high-tech equipment may not be a justifiable variance.

Structured budgeting processes can help develop and advance a ministry, while sloppy budgeting can blindside a church and affect the long-term viability of the ministry. When finances get out of control, it creates the necessity to take drastic measures to get things back on track. And that's not something anyone in leadership wants to do.

Without tithing congregants, there are no revenues to budget. For this reason, target strategic plans and budgets at one thing and one thing only: the customers. This is why it's imperative to identify the donors, find out what they want (within the mission and vision of the church) and put systems and processes in place to meet their needs.

Budgeting and allocating resources is a very challenging task. A number of things compete for budgeted dollars, which can make the processes overwhelming and difficult to prioritize. Having a good prioritization model for budget decision-making can take some of the guesswork out of such decisions.

Department managers often get requests for the newest software, the newest phones and gadgets, the most recent model of office equipment, etc. Without a streamlined process to prioritize decisions, managers can end up wasting valuable budget dollars on things that don't add value or advance the organization.

So what are some things a manager needs to consider when making a budgetary decision?

Base all spending and budgeting decisions on a simple decision model by asking these questions. Is this expenditure a:

Want—something that would make the job easier

Need—something that's important to get the job accomplished

Have-to-Have—something that's necessary for the success of the operation

For example, a new version of a software program is available. The question then is this, "Is this something we want, we need, or we have-to-have?" Most likely, the purchase can probably wait even though it may make the job easier.

However, if the copy machine goes down and putting together handouts for the children's ministry is part of the daily operation, this request would fall into the have-to-have category.

This expenditure affects the success of the operation, so the resources need to be available.

Are there budget dollars available to spend? As part of the budgeting process, budget dollars specifically for emergency expenditures that cover the have-to-have spending decisions. If there are no budgeted dollars available, are there other budgets to modify to free up available dollars? For example, if there are dollars allocated for a special event, are there ways to cut some of those costs so some of those dollars can go toward something else, or are there budgeted overtime hours that free up resources for something else?

Does the spending line up with church goals, and, ultimately, will the spending get the ministry closer to the vision? For example, a conference comes up that isn't budgeted. The question to ask is, "Will this conference help better equip the staff for completion of departmental goals?" If not, even if dollars are available, it may be best not to spend them.

As managers, we face spending decisions every day, and unless we have a good foundation for decision-making, we can easily overspend budget dollars.

Managing a budget is a skill that all managers need to learn. Part of that skill is having a good understanding of where the organization is going so that they make all spending decisions in accordance with the vision and strategic plan.

Embezzlement

I was saddened to read about a neighborhood church, where my kids used to attend youth events, being yet another victim of church embezzlement. All you have to do is go to your search bar and type in "church embezzlement," and you'll find many headlines:

- Woman pleads guilty to embezzling $300 from church
- Manlius church treasurer's husband arraigned on embezzlement charges
- Treasurer convicted and sentenced for embezzling over $110,000 from church bank accounts in California
- Church bookkeeper gets three years for embezzlement
- Largest South Korean church's embezzlement scandal just got worse

And the list goes on. According to Brotherhood Mutual Insurance Company, "Church crime continues to grow—estimated at $100 million each day. Increasing at an annual rate of nearly 6 percent, researchers expect church financial fraud to reach the $60 billion mark by 2025."

With about 80 percent of all cases of church fraud being unreported, this is staggering! So what the heck is going on? Are churches really this mismanaged?

The concept of a trusted bookkeeper, treasurer, or money counter stealing from the church is simply counter-intuitive for those of us who embrace Christian principles.

We are the church. We trust people, we love people, and we give people the benefit of the doubt. That's what we do.

The reality check, for church leaders, is the realization that easy access, no controls, and personal need (or justification) are all stepping stones to church fraud.

We all want to believe that the sweet lady who diligently keeps the books would never steal, but the reality is if the conditions are right, embezzlement is inevitable, and once it begins, it becomes a slippery slope.

It starts small, maybe one of the counters slips $10 into his pocket, no one finds out, and then it becomes a little easier to muster up the nerve to do it again. No one finds out, so they try again. These examples are merely holes in the armor and demonstrate a lack of management and control.

10 Practices that Safeguard Against Church Embezzlement

1. Policy and Procedures

The first step in any effort of control is to write policies and procedures. Spend some time thinking through how your organization would like to control the handling of, and access to, church funds.

Clearly state policies for things like cash-handling, two-person accountability, rotation of counters, and a commitment to auditing, to name just a few. The more eyes on the books, the more likely it is for someone to notice irregularities.

2. Training

Require employees and volunteers who help with counting the offering, or assisting in the church office, to attend annual training on proper cash-handling. Include in this training the measures that the ministry takes to safeguard its financial resources. This simple step will make would-be perpetrators think twice because they will see the organization is diligent in its efforts to protect its resources.

3. Audits

Church audits are expensive, there's no question, but it's critical that the church takes the steps to conduct thorough church audits on a regular basis.

Have an independent outside auditor do these audits. This is another step that alerts the potential thief that someone reviews the books and will discover misappropriation of funds.

4. Rotation

Rotate volunteers and employees who help with counting the offering on a regular basis. No one should stay in the role indefinitely and the use of multiple, unrelated people will make it more difficult to skim dollars from the offering.

5. Safes

Keep cash and checks securely in a locked safe until it's time to deliver them to the bank. Get a safe with a drop slot so that it doesn't require someone to open it to make a deposit.

Have a policy that only two people open the safe and limit the combination to a few people who do not have a key to the room with the safe. These simple security measures will help to control your risk.

6. Two-Person Rule

The cash-handling policy should have a strict two-person rule. The rule says there's always a minimum of two people when handling, counting, and transporting cash. The two people are unrelated, and they must not have personal financial issues.

7. Background/Credit Checks

In today's society, it's wise to perform a background check on all church employees and volunteers. Additionally, do a credit check on people who have access to church funds. While this practice may seem a little invasive, this simple step can provide information that can ultimately protect the church. As with all sensitive information, use strict confidentiality practices.

8. Watch for Warning Signs

There are many signs you can watch for, but a few to think about are:

- Only one person has access to offering, cash, checks, and check log.
- Person with access doesn't take vacations and guards against someone else doing the job.

- Person with access is living beyond their means.
- Person with access has personal financial issues.
- It's difficult to get a financial summary from the responsible person.
- There's inadequate supervision of person(s) handling cash.

9. Act on Suspicion

If you have a gut feeling, take the time to investigate and act on your instincts. Solicit help from a trained fraud examiner to help you sort through your suspicions.

10. Supervision/Management

Church leaders are responsible for managing operational practices within the church. Whether that oversight is of employees or volunteers, it's critical to have good supervision of those who deal with church funds.

Our natural leadership tendency is to empower people with the freedom to work independently, but when it comes to church finances, throw that leadership principle out the window.

Enforce the practice of keeping church financial records in the church office. Make your presence known, ask questions and insist on timely financial reporting. Management and supervision are crucial aspects of financial controls.

Churches could not exist without the generous support of its members. Those who embrace the Christian principle of giving, trust that church leaders will be good stewards of their donations.

These countless cases of church fraud and embezzlement speak to the critical need for church boards and leadership to wake up, do their job, and safeguard God's money. I challenge you today to call a meeting and discuss this critical issue with your leadership team.

CHAPTER 7

Paid Labor

"When the righteous are in authority, the people rejoice;
But when a wicked man rules, the people groan."
Proverbs 29:2

Hiring Staff

Managing the human resource function of a church is every bit as challenging as managing people in a business setting. A church is only as strong as the people it employs, and weak employees can affect the ability of the church to flourish and meet objectives. As Jim Collins states in Good to Great:

> "Get the right people on the bus, the wrong people off the bus, the right people in the right seats and then figure out where to drive."

Employing the right people requires a great strategy to recruit, screen, interview, orient, and train new employees. Each step of the hiring process can affect the ability to select the right candidate so a structured process and consistency in practice is important.

Employee Recruitment

It requires focused strategy to recruit the best and brightest for the ministry.

Recruiting a church employee can be a challenge because of the political aspect of hiring someone from within the congregation. There needs to be a structured recruitment and screening process coupled with great communication to avoid the inevitable offense that comes when congregants apply to work for their church and don't get hired.

Good communication coupled with a great interview process is the best way to guard against this. Recruiting outside the congregation can increase the talent pool, but it may be more difficult to find someone who supports the mission of the church, which should be a requirement for every church employee.

The HR Council should set guidelines for how to manage recruitment and determine whether the church should focus on hiring from within the congregation or use outside resources to identify the right person for the job. There are different schools of thought on this, which is why a church leadership group should discuss pros and cons of each method and then determine the best approach.

Hiring Process

The HR Council is also responsible for creating a hiring process that includes recruitment strategies, interviews, testing, background checks, orientation, and job training.

It's important to have a structured and streamlined process to ensure screening new employees for the best fit.

It's far better to delay a hiring decision than to hire the wrong person—no matter how desperate the need is to fill the position!

Streamline the hiring process with a structured communication procedure for job applicants. Consider applicants a customer group and give the courtesy of consistent and clear communication. Anticipating the kind of information a job applicant might need and building a process around that is the best approach.

For example, when someone applies for a job, send an acknowledgement letter immediately to let the applicant know that the church received the application. Communicate with the applicant at three critical steps:

- When the application is received
- When an interview is scheduled
- When the position is filled, whether the applicant got the job or not

Part of the communication is setting the expectations for when the applicant might hear back. It's common courtesy to let applicants know they're no longer in the running for the job, which also helps to avoid awkward follow-up phone calls.

For instance, if it's common for several people to review applications before scheduling an interview and that process typically takes weeks or even months, let the applicant know so there's a realistic expectation for when he or she might hear about the job.

If things change and the process will take a little longer, let the applicant know. Always err on the side of too much communication. Just think about what kind of information you would appreciate if you were the applicant and then act on it.

Screening

Getting to know some things about a potential employee before bringing that person onboard is an important step and requires running background checks and calling references. Every organization should have an identified vendor to run background checks.

Running background checks is no longer a luxury but a necessity in the hiring process. This is especially true for church staff who may have access to children. Most insurance companies can refer you to a reputable organization that does this kind of screening.

Checking personal references is another great way to find out information about a potential employee.

Verifying the reference's relationship with the candidate and asking some general questions can flush out valuable information. Taking the time to make these kinds of phone calls can help ensure the candidate is the right fit for the organization.

Interviewing

Hiring employees can be scary for churches because the decision to enter into an employer/employee relationship can affect the church and its ability to fulfill its mission. If the right person is chosen, it can mean doing additional things more quickly. However, if it's the wrong person, it can result in management challenges, frustrations, and distraction from focusing on those mission critical objectives.

A mistake many churches make is to hire faithful members without taking into consideration their skill sets, work ethic but, more importantly, their calling. Very often people get confused about the difference between answering the call to help a church in a volunteer capacity and the unique calling that comes with being a church employee. Confusing the two can mean hiring the wrong person.

This can result in the stressful termination of a faithful member and volunteer. These types of situations often result in offense and don't always end well.

> "But select from among you, brethren, seven men of good reputation, full of the Spirit and of wisdom, whom we may put in charge of this task." Acts 6:3

You need to consider several things while you prepare for that new hire.

- Make sure you have an updated job description that defines the explicit skills required to perform the job. Take some time to review this document so you know the specific job questions to ask.

- If the candidate is a church member, find out what volunteer jobs they've held, what discipleship programs they've participated in and their level of commitment to the mission.
- If the hire is to replace a current employee, take some time to consider the person vacating the job and reflect on those characteristics he or she had that enhanced or took away from job performance.
- Study the candidate's application and resume so you can ask questions about work history and job skills. Specifically, look for what they did that can help the church fulfill its mission.
- If the person will fill a position to answer the telephone, a phone interview might be appropriate to test how well the candidate communicates on the phone.
- Have a list of prepared interview questions and select questions that are appropriate for the job and position level of the candidate. You will more than likely ask a manager different questions from those you would a receptionist.
- Set an agenda and use an interview guide to help keep you focused.

It isn't always easy to carve out this necessary preparation time, but doing so can have a significant impact on the outcome of the interview process.

As you filter through resumes look for:

Job Qualifications—You want to make sure the candidate meets the basic qualifications for the job. If the job requires a college degree, then look at the educational background to see whether the candidate can meet those requirements.

Tenure—Pay attention to the length of time an employee stays with a job. If a candidate changes jobs every year or two, it may be an indication of unknown job issues.

Key Accomplishments—While it's vital to look at formal education, it's also important to look for key accomplishments. Specifically, what did the employee contribute to the organization? A formal education does not necessarily indicate someone's ability to contribute and create value.

Red Flags—Look for those things that might indicate a poor employment history, things like gaps in employment, a career that has plateaued or gone backwards, short tenure, or having several jobs in a short period of time, or a career path that has taken multiple shifts.

You've weeded through the resumes, selected a few candidates to interview and now it's time to meet them and have a conversation. Make sure you have a list of questions that will help you to determine the candidate's calling, skill set and ability to meet the job requirements.

Interviewing is a skill that develops only with practice, but preparing for the interview is an important first step. Knowing the right questions to ask is critical to identifying the right person for the job.The goal of interview questions is to get to know the candidate, so get them talking, sharing, and expressing themselves.

When hiring for a church, there are some foundational characteristics you want to look for in job candidates:

Spiritual Maturity—Working in a church environment isn't always easy, and having a high level of spiritual maturity can help employees deal with the inevitable challenges that come with working for a church.

> "Like newborn babies, crave pure spiritual milk, so that by it you may grow up in your salvation...." 1 Peter 2:2

Calling—Working for a church is a calling, making it an important to determine who receives the call to the ministry and who is merely looking for employment. Taking the time to find the person who has the calling to do the job will result in the best employee.

> "Now may the God of peace, who through the blood of the eternal covenant brought back from the dead our Lord

> Jesus, that great Shepherd of the sheep, equip you with everything good for doing His will, and may He work in us what is pleasing to Him, through Jesus Christ...." Hebrews 13:20-21

Personal Character—People who work for a church set the standard for behavior and require honesty and integrity.

> "He must also have a good reputation with outsiders, so that he will not fall into disgrace and into the devil's trap." 1 Timothy 3:7

Faithfulness—Church employees should be loyal to the church and its mission. They should understand that their faithfulness ties to their ability to support the church mission.

> "Like the cold of snow in the time of harvest is a faithful messenger to those who send him; he refreshes the soul of his masters." Proverbs 25:13

Skill Set—Employees need to have the aptitude and skills to do the job, but they also need to pursue personal development and work toward increased and improved skills.

> "Let every skillful craftsman among you come and make all that the Lord has commanded." Exodus 35:10

Submission—Employees need to submit to and respect authority. Rebellious employees cause problems, distractions, and undue stress.

> "Let every person be subject to the governing authorities. For there is no authority except from God, and those that exist have been instituted by God." Romans 13:1

Work Ethic—There are a lot of submissive employees with the right skill set, and even calling, who lack work ethic. Determining someone's ability to get the job done is important to finding that right person.

> "One who is faithful in a very little is also faithful in much, and one who is dishonest in a very little is also dishonest in much." Luke 16:10

Now let's go over some possible questions to ask that can help you to identify candidates with these important characteristics.

1. Please tell me what makes you interested in working for this church? Calling
2. What makes you interested in this particular job? Calling
3. What is your understanding of our mission and vision and what we're trying to accomplish? Faithfulness/calling
4. Tell me what you do in your current position? Skill set
5. Tell me about a time you identified an improvement opportunity for your current employer. Work ethic
6. Describe the best boss you've ever had. Submission
7. Describe the most difficult boss you've ever had. Submission/ spiritual maturity/character
8. If I called your boss today, how would he describe you as an employee? Work ethic/character
9. What would your boss say your strengths are? Skill set
10. What did your boss say at your last performance appraisal? Work ethic/character
11. Tell me about a time when your supervisor coached you on performance. Submission/spiritual maturity/character
12. What are your personal growth opportunities? Skill set/ spiritual maturity
13. What is your personal approach to conflict resolution? Spiritual maturity/character
14. Tell me about a time you had conflict with a coworker and how you resolved it. Spiritual maturity/character

15. Can you tell me the different ways you spend time with God?
    Spiritual maturity

Being prepared for new hires by reviewing the candidate's resume and using these interview questions can help to facilitate an effective interview conversation. However, as important as all of the preparation, screening, and interviews are, nothing will help you to identify that God-appointed employee like prayer. Make sure you and your team spend time praying for God's wisdom for every person you hire!

> "If any of you lacks wisdom, you should ask God, who gives generously to all without finding fault, and it will be given to you." James 1:5

Interviewing mistakes managers make

- Hiring someone who's like you, often done unconsciously.
- Not probing on answers. Keep asking questions for clarification until you get the full answer.
- Asking hypothetical questions. This allows the candidate to give answers that may not necessarily reflect his typical approach to problem-solving.
- Asking leading questions. These can take a candidate down a road she would not otherwise have traveled.
- Hiring on first impression. If you make up your mind early in the interview that you like the person, you're not as likely to probe and give the interview the full focus it deserves.
- Hiring on gut feeling. Our gut feelings are sometimes accurate, but often they're wrong. Make sure you base hiring decisions on objective data obtained from the interview process. But, most importantly, seek God's guidance on all hiring decisions.

Interviewing job candidates is a developed skill. Taking the necessary time to prepare for an interview is the best way to practice and develop that skill. Getting to know the job candidate through interview questions improves the likelihood the candidate will work well within the organization.

Employee Orientation

When employees are new to an organization, they must go through an orientation process. The person who has responsibility for the HR function typically does this. Small organizations that don't hire people frequently, like larger organizations, don't usually have systems and processes in place to ensure a smooth orientation process. A simple solution is to create a new employee orientation checklist to use the first days or weeks after hiring a new employee.

To create a new employee orientation checklist, simply gather a group of employees and ask them, what kind of information was important for them to know when they were first hired. Going through the new employee orientation check sheet is a shared responsibility of the person responsible for the HR function and the hiring manager.

Here are some examples of things that could be part of a new employee orientation:

- ✓ Review of policies
- ✓ Employee policies
- ✓ Office hours
- ✓ Employee benefits
- ✓ Vacation request process
- ✓ Who to call when sick
- ✓ Office tour
- ✓ Office/campus tour—i.e., where to find coffee, where to eat lunch
- ✓ How to use the phone system, retrieve voicemail, etc.
- ✓ Lunchroom (the unwritten rules)

- ✓ Where to find office supplies
- ✓ Where to find mail
- ✓ Keys to facility
- ✓ How to operate office machines—for example, the copy machine
- ✓ How to log in to the computer
- ✓ Any pertinent passwords
- ✓ Compensation process
- ✓ When is payday
- ✓ How are hours tracked and recorded
- ✓ Health insurance
- ✓ Retirement contribution
- ✓ Overtime
- ✓ Lunch/break times
- ✓ General
- ✓ Organizational chart
- ✓ Confidentiality
- ✓ Staff meeting schedule
- ✓ Computer passwords
- ✓ Voicemail etiquette
- ✓ Email etiquette
- ✓ What are the social norms (unwritten rules) of the organization? For example, are employees expected to hang out together at lunch?
- ✓ Customer service expectations (congregants, volunteers, other employees)
- ✓ Department orientation

- ✓ Department chain-of-command
- ✓ Performance management process
- ✓ Employee job description
- ✓ Employee goals
- ✓ Team expectations
- ✓ Employee mentor
- ✓ Meet coworkers

Complete and sign this kind of checklist within seven days of the hire date and maintain it in the department and employee file.

The human resource function for a church has many of the same legal requirements as other organizations and should have a designated person with responsibility and goals assigned to these job tasks.

The Society for Human Resources (www.shrm.org) is a great organization that offers resources and training for this critical role.

Job Training

It's important the ministry provides the necessary training for new employees. This may be training on the telephone system, email system, and any other software the employee will work on. This should include identifying a new-employee mentor who can answer any questions the employee has. New employees very often try to figure things out rather than ask questions, so having an assigned person to help the new employee will ensure a great start to the work experience.

Job Description

Providing employees with a detailed job description is the best way to prepare them for a successful employment experience. As described in Chapter 2, job descriptions should reflect expected tasks and responsibilities of the role and should be updated annually to ensure that changing focuses and priorities are in the job description.

The reporting supervisor should explain the job description and lay out expectations for performance clearly as well as the consequences for not meeting expectations. Poor stewardship allows employees to continue to perform tasks that may no longer be relevant to strategy and goals.

Managing Church Staff

Having worked for a church for 10 years, I have a good understanding of the unique challenges that church employees face. Working for a ministry is different from working for any other type of organization in that it requires some spiritual resilience and self-preservation skills.

I have a quote written in the back of my Bible (unfortunately, I didn't note who said it) but the quote goes like this:

"Don't get so caught up in the ministry of the Lord that we forget the Lord of the ministry."

Church staff is unique in that they facilitate the process of weekly services as well as church events. They're the ones who make sure the doors get unlocked and the building is clean, stocked, and prepared for the congregation. They're the ones who prepare the music, organize the volunteers, and support the pastor. Very often, these responsibilities overshadow the "worship" experience.

Church employees need to have an extra layer of spiritual armor so they can fulfill their responsibilities while maintaining their relationship with God.

Employees are one of the three church customer groups, and church leadership should make it a priority to support those people who devote their lives to the furtherance of the Gospel.

Church leaders should have a deliberate plan to encourage and support employees. There are many things they can do to support church staff.

Things That Can Help Keep a Church Staff Energized and Engaged

Time with God

One day, when I was struggling as a church staff member, I heard God whisper these words: "You need to do the things you did that got you to where you are." It was an amazing revelation of the importance of continuing to nurture my personal relationship with God.

Those who are responsible for overseeing church staff should make sure employees take the necessary time to nurture their own relationship with the Father. This is critical to the effectiveness and endurance of church staff.

The church I worked for had a designated pastoral-led noon hour of prayer and invited all staff to participate. This model facilitated an opportunity for prayer during work hours.

Time with Self

Vibrant churches have a lot going on, and the opportunities for participation are endless. Encourage staff to prioritize those things they're involved with so they have ample time to rest, refresh, and recharge.

Time with family and friends is an important part of refreshing and recharging. Churches should provide ample paid time off so employees can pace their efforts for the long haul. Worn out and exhausted employees are not as productive or enthusiastic as those who have ample rest and time to recharge, so helping them maintain a healthy work-life balance is important.

Keep the Vision in Front of Them

Keeping the vision in front of people is a great responsibility and is critical to keeping employees focused on priorities and those things that support the vision. Remind employees of where the church was, where it currently is, and where it's going, and the importance of their role in helping to fulfill the mission. When employees understand how what they do supports church strategy, they feel more connected to their jobs and engaged in their work.

Keep Employees Engaged

It's important for employees to feel as if they're making a difference. When employees feel engaged, they put their hearts and souls into their work and maintain the excitement and energy to perform job duties.

Unengaged employees merely go through the motions. They may perform job tasks but lack the spark to perform at their best and to make a significant difference. Employees have a direct impact on the customer experience, making engagement so critical.

These are some things that organizations with strong cultures of employee engagement do well. The organization has a strong vision that employees understand and feel connected to. Also, there's consistent and strategic communication that helps employees understand the church's unique challenges, opportunities, and accomplishments.

There's a lot of research that suggests employees leave organizations not because of their jobs but because of their direct supervisors. Manager interaction with staff is a critical part of employee engagement. This includes how well managers share information, how they interact with employees, how the employee perceives equity, and how managers care for employees as individuals.

Staff Development—Employees want to know there are developmental opportunities to grow in their jobs and within the organization.

Compensation and Benefits—People work on a church staff because of the calling and not for monetary gain.

Most church employees recognize that people tithe to pay their salaries and understand the importance of responsible stewardship of God's money. However, it's only right for church employees to have a fair and competitive salary for the same tasks and responsibilities as others who work on church staffs. There are some great resources available online that benchmark church staff salaries and benefits based on church size and revenues.

> "...Do not withhold good from those to whom it is due,
> when it is in the power of your hand to do so..."
> Proverbs 3:27 NKJV

A structured performance management process incorporates merit increases into an annual cycle based on performance appraisals and goal completion. Employees should have a good understanding of what's expected of them and what the rewards are for meeting expectations.

They should never have to wonder about when they will get raises or what they need to do to perform well. Communication every step of the way helps keep employees engaged. The secret is to create a process and stick to it. For example, if raises are in January, the performance appraisal and goal development process should begin in September or October to allow ample time for feedback and performance appraisal development.

Tips for Being a Great Manager

Anyone who has ever held a management position understands the challenges that come with managing employees. Managers have the responsibility to help employees develop job skills, and they also hold employees accountable for completing jobs. Being in a management position requires an aptitude for dealing with the many diverse aspects of interacting with employees. A great manager cares about the employee on a personal level as well as the employee's ability to accomplish key responsibilities.

Traits of a Great Manager

Excellent Communicator—Good communication is the secret to success for any organization. Managers should make communicating with employees a priority and constantly ask themselves, "What is it that I know my employees may need to know"? Then tell them!

Employees have an interest in the organization and have a desire to know what's new, what's changing, and what news will affect their jobs. Talk to them and they will appreciate it!

Builds Great Teams—Building strong teams is what creates a productive work environment, and managers should demonstrate team leader skills. A good manager can take a random group of people and transform them into a collective unit that collaborates, works toward a shared goal, and enjoys the process.

Influential Leader—Effective leaders inspire and influence the behavior of others. Managers should demonstrate leadership skills to gain employee respect and confidence. Managers need to be consistent with what they say and what they do. This helps to engage and gain employee trust. Employees want to work for managers with good moral character that they demonstrate by personal ethical behavior.

Nurturing Mentor/Coach—Every employee is on a developmental journey, and managers have the responsibility of mentoring and coaching them. They do this by taking the time to find those teachable moments and helping the employee think through appropriate responses to the work environment.

For example, my daughter is a young professional who works for a large Fortune 500 company. She had a coworker who was constantly criticizing her publicly and embarrassing her in front of her peers. She chose not to do anything about it because she doesn't like conflict.

Her manager witnessed a few of these events, called my daughter into her office, instructed her to confront the employee privately, and gave her some tips for how to do it and what to say. My daughter was terrified but followed through as instructed, and the situation was resolved.

These seemingly insignificant occurrences, if not addressed, can have a great impact on the work environment and, more importantly, on the employee's professional development.

Capture these teachable moments as opportunities for managers to mentor and coach employees. I raise my hat to the woman who manages my daughter. She recognized the importance of encouraging her to stretch out of her comfort zone. This not only resolved the issue but also helped my daughter grow professionally!

Effective Time Management—There are never enough hours in the day, and there are always unpredictable curve balls that derail the best of time managers. A key management competency is one that finds efficiency in work time and helps employees with managing their time at work. Chit chatting in the hallway for 15 minutes here and there is a time thief that most organizations don't have the luxury for. Identify those things that steal valuable time and work to eliminate them.

Sets Measurable Goals—Goals are how to meet objectives and to accomplish a mission. Managers need to write measurable goals that support the strategy and mission of the church and help employees do the same.

Provides Feedback—All too often, managers get frustrated with employees for not performing up to their expectations, when the reality is, they failed to communicate what it was that they expected from them. Managers have the responsibility of providing consistent, unbiased feedback. They need to hear when they're doing things well, and they also need to know about those times when they're not meeting expectations.

Fair and Unbiased—We all come to the workplace from different backgrounds and with unconscious biases due to our individual experiences. An effective manager can identify those personal biases and not allow them to influence how to manage employees. Maintaining objectivity when dealing with employees is imperative to fair management practices.

Managing employees can be one of the most rewarding experiences anyone can have, and there's nothing more fulfilling than watching an employee develop professional acumen. Some managers try to manage the time that employees are at work, but effective managers are skilled at managing the people, which ultimately develops the person and produces results.

CHAPTER 8

Free Labor

"Your people shall be volunteers in the
day of Your power." Psalms 110:3 NKJV

Free Labor

The beauty of a church community is the abundance of committed people who have an interest in helping the church achieve its vision and mission. Volunteers provide free labor and are an important part of any ministry.

They are the ones who play the music, usher in visitors, and take care of the children, and so on. Providing good volunteer support helps to create a positive experience for those people who give of their time. This support begins with a volunteer management model that consistently looks for ways to improve the volunteer experience.

The church exists to equip God's saints and has a responsibility to develop the saints in their walk so that every believer can fulfill the individual plan God has for his or her life. We accomplish much of this development through volunteer opportunities. Many people use the volunteer experience to get to know other members in the church community and grow in their walk with God.

Effective volunteer management incorporates many things that contribute to a positive experience for the volunteer.

12 Things Volunteers Expect

1. Organization

We all know that some people are more organized than others, but most would agree that everyone appreciates organized systems and processes because they make our lives easier.

Think about going to the doctor's office and, buried under piles of paper, the clerk behind the desk can't seem to find the paperwork for your visit. Or go to a lender to sign loan papers, and the employee digs pieces of paper from here and there trying to gather all of the documents. This kind of disorder frustrates everyone and doesn't elicit confidence in the process.

2. Good Use of Time

Volunteers generously give of their time but want to use that time wisely. When volunteers show up for a scheduled shift, they want to be productive and make their time count. This requires not only ensuring there are enough people to do a project but also that there are enough job tasks to keep those people busy while they're there.

Think through all job duties and make sure volunteers know what to do by providing a volunteer job description and the approximate time it will take to accomplish the task. Overestimating or underestimating the time it will take to accomplish a task can have a negative effect, but if you err on the side of overestimating the time needed, volunteers may finish sooner than expected and have the option of going home early.

When things take longer than planned, it can conflict with other commitments volunteers have and possibly make them think twice the next time there's an opportunity to help. For example, three volunteers are going to plant flowers around the church campus. The supervisor asks them to work from 9:00 a.m. to noon. When they arrive, have someone there waiting for them with all the supplies (plants, gloves, hand shovel, mulch, etc) staged and ready to go.

If the volunteers show up and no one is there to greet them, it could result in wasting valuable (free labor) time. In addition to its wasting time, it can also result in having a negative impact on the volunteer experience.

But if someone eagerly greets the volunteers and puts them to work upon arrival, they benefit from the good feeling that comes with accomplishing something significant for the church. Hence—a good use of their time!

3. Clear Expectations

Good communication on the front end can eliminate lots of unnecessary issues on the back end. Communicating what you expect helps volunteers succeed. Volunteers donate their time, and someone needs to provide clear job expectations, a detailed volunteer job description, and orientation to the organization.

Volunteers are very much like employees in that when they come to work, they want a clear understanding of the expectations. The more clear and concise the direction the more comfortable the volunteers are in completing their assigned tasks. For example, a volunteer might have to empty trashcans during an event.

Vague expectations: "You're assigned to emptying the trash cans." Clear expectations: "You're assigned to emptying the trash cans around the campus. There are 15 cans located here (show on map). Please empty them once an hour and take the full bags of trash to the dumpster on the back side of the building (show on map).

The trash bags and gloves are in the janitor's closet (show on map). If you have any questions or perhaps need help with a heavy can, please go to the information booth and have them radio the setup team leader whose name is Jack. Do you have any questions?"

The more detail you can provide volunteers helps in two ways. It answers questions before they think to ask them, and it eliminates having multiple people ask the same questions during an event. A clear job description, training on job duties, and a mentor (go-to person) are critical to this.

4. Provide the Tools and Training to Perform Job Tasks

It's important to provide a positive experience for volunteers to ensure they enjoy their assigned job. Volunteers need to understand what it takes to perform their jobs and have the necessary tools or equipment. For example, an usher who will distribute offering envelopes needs to know where to find them, or it could potentially create a frustrating experience.

Volunteer training should include information about where needed supplies and equipment are and who the go-to person is for questions. Whether a volunteer is supposed to work in the nursery, usher, or greet guests, there's a basic expectation they will receive the necessary training to do their tasks.

This includes a global understanding of the church, specific departmental training, and job-specific training.

Cover all three areas to ensure the volunteer is comfortable performing their job duties. For example, if a volunteer is to work in the nursery, he or she will need training on sanitation procedures, drop off/pick up procedures, child discipline protocol, emergency response protocols before beginning the first shift. Proper volunteer training helps them feel confident in completing their job duties and fosters a great worker experience.

5. Involved in the Process

Church volunteers are those people who are committed to the organization and have a passion for its mission. Because of this, they have an interest in the systems and processes that make church happen. Allowing volunteers to share thoughts, ideas, and opinions helps them feel valued and keeps them engaged. For example, if a volunteer works in the nursery and has the opportunity to offer suggestions on improving how to minister to the children, they feel valued and involved in the organization. In addition, the volunteers who do the day-to-day jobs often have great ideas for improvement.

6. Feel Appreciated

Recognizing a volunteer's contribution and showing appreciation is critical to volunteer oversight.

Volunteers give many hours of free labor and have a basic expectation that there's some level of appreciation for what they do. This can be something as simple as a handwritten thank you note to an elaborate recognition at an annual volunteer banquet.

Regardless, taking the time to think about what volunteers contribute and acknowledge their commitment goes a long way in making them feel valued. There are many volunteer management systems that track volunteer hours worked, which provides great data that can help you recognize volunteer efforts.

7. Part of a Team

Church members volunteer for many reasons, but one of the biggest motivators is the sense of community that comes with working with other congregants. Feeling like you're part of a team is a major motivator for people and providing the environment that fosters that social interaction is key to a positive experience.

8. Care About Them as People

Whether the volunteer is new to the church or is a long-term member, everyone wants to know they are cared about on a personal level.

Volunteers love when they are encouraged to talk about their family and their personal lives and when church leadership takes an interest in them. This sense of belonging helps to foster relationships that are invaluable in times of personal crisis.

9. Consistent Communication

I'm a firm believer that there can never be too much communication. We often experience information overload, but volunteers appreciate consistent flows of information. We do this by creating a predictable and consistent communication process so volunteers know when to expect what kinds of information. For instance, volunteer schedules can be done monthly, quarterly, or annually; it doesn't matter. What does matter is ensuring that the volunteer knows when to expect the schedule in the mail.

If the communication and information flow is unpredictable, the volunteer may not receive the needed information in a timely manner. Learn to communicate when and how to share information. This helps them to prepare, and the supervisor can do this as part of the volunteer orientation process.

10. Fix What's Broken

Volunteers are the hands and feet of the church and are down in the trenches doing the work.

Therefore, they have a good understanding of what's working and what's not. These workers appreciate when they have the opportunity to point out needy areas and assurances that someone will fix them.

For example, volunteers in the parking ministry may use radio headsets to communicate to each other. If a worker says that some of the equipment is malfunctioning, reassure them that someone will fix it within a reasonable amount of time.

Employees and volunteers alike should have the (functioning) tools to perform their job duties. Fix the problems that cause worker frustration and make job assignments easier.

11. Follow Through on Promises Made

Leaders build credibility on what they say and what they do. This means every area of leadership but specifically on promises made. When an organization makes a promise to do something, employees and volunteers expect someone to follow up on that promise, and if things change, they expect someone to tell them why there was a change.

12. Error-Free Process, Documents, and Follow Through

Volunteers enjoy helping an organization that takes pride in everything it does, and the church builds its credibility on creating and maintaining a professional environment. Volunteers and church members alike appreciate churches that commit to quality and excellence by continually improving their systems and processes and striving for professionalism, not perfection. This includes things like a volunteer application that's free from errors and typos or a streamlined, efficient application process.

For example, a volunteer just completes a volunteer application, gets a phone call interview and asking about job interests, and the interviewer says he or she will receive a schedule in a welcome packet within a week. Three or four weeks go by, and the volunteer doesn't hear anything and wonders what happened. It's important for systems to support a positive experience. The volunteer department is responsible for making sure that volunteer interactions are positive and that it makes every effort to provide an efficient, error-free, and responsible communication to the volunteer.

Volunteer labor is the engine of any church, ministry, or nonprofit.

Thinking about what volunteers need and expect in exchange for their time commitment is an important step in making sure they have a satisfying volunteer experience. Talking to volunteers and asking how the organization can improve their experience is one of the best ways to flush this information out. Meeting the expectations of this valuable group of people can go a long way in recruiting and retaining a church's free labor force.

Good volunteer management is critical to the success of any ministry since many churches don't have the resources for paid staff and rely heavily on volunteer labor. Successful churches have systems and processes in place to oversee and manage volunteers to ensure a great worker experience and volunteers perform the jobs correctly. A well-run volunteer program creates the infrastructure to support volunteer management and creates a process to facilitate efficient volunteer oversight.

Volunteer Orientation

A structured orientation process helps to prepare the volunteer for his/her new job responsibilities. Volunteers need to have a working knowledge of the church history—where it has been and what it hopes to achieve.

So what should volunteer orientation cover?

History of the Church

People who attend the same church for a long time can typically recite the church's history. New volunteers should know when and how the church started and any milestones it achieved along the way. Sharing pertinent statistics like how many people attended the first service, where the early services were as compared to current membership, and the progression of the church gives volunteers a historical perspective and helps them to connect to the church body.

Mission, Vision, and Values

The mission, vision, and values of a church are what steers its direction, so it's important for volunteers to understand why the church exists, where it has been, where it currently is, and what it hopes to achieve. This kind of information helps to connect the volunteer to the church mission in an intimate way.

Information about the Pastor(s)

New volunteers should know who the pastors in the church are, where they have been prior to serving this church, where they went to school, information about their family, and what responsibilities they have in the church.

This helps give the volunteer a guide for knowing which pastor to ask for additional information and for addressing church-related issues.

Church Culture

Every organization has a culture that affects the way it communicates information, how it makes decisions, and how people interact with each other.

Giving a synopsis of church culture helps the volunteer understand the unwritten rules of behavior. For example, if the church is very traditional, the culture may be less tolerant of talking in church than one that's a little more relaxed and contemporary. The goal is to help the volunteer understand the behavioral norms.

Do's and Don'ts of Volunteers

Everyone comes from a different background and has a different frame of reference and life experiences. Because volunteers represent the church, they should have specific instruction on expected behaviors.

Here's an example. A volunteer is supposed to report for a job at the scheduled time (do), but a volunteer should not park in the reserved parking area (don't).

During orientation and in the church volunteer job description, it's important to communicate as much information as possible to make sure the volunteer understands expectations and to minimize volunteer issues when he or she violated an unwritten rule.

Customer Service Standards

Anyone who works in a service industry understands the concept of customer service standards. A church volunteer is no different. And, should become familiar with the expectations for serving church customers (other volunteers, staff, or congregation).

Reviewing these standards helps the volunteer understand the basic service expectations. People who have never had service training can benefit from basic customer service principles like these:

- Who are the customers? What do they want? How do we meet their needs?
- Be polite.
- Give people the benefit of the doubt.
- If you're not sure what to do, do what's right for the customer.

Example: Service Standards

Anticipate customer needs by identifying expectations and working toward meeting those needs.

For example, if an usher sees someone enter the church in a wheelchair, the usher should actively help that person find a wheelchair-friendly spot.

Exceed expectations of all customer groups. For example, a door greeter who sees someone approaching the building will open the door for the person and extend a greeting.

Hold ourselves accountable for organizational service commitment. For instance, when working in a volunteer capacity, be constantly aware of the service responsibility in the role.

Be aware of communication style and always communicate professionally. Be sensitive to eye contact and tone of voice. For example, when a children's church worker is welcoming a new parent, the worker should communicate with a smile and good eye contact to give that parent reassurance that the child is in good hands.

Listen to customer requests and take immediate action to fulfill the requests. For example, if the restroom attendant gets a request from a visitor for hand lotion, the volunteer should quickly try to find it for the visitor. Keep customers informed of any delays in service. For example, if the restroom volunteer can't find hand lotion, she should tell the visitor.

Greet all customers in a professional and courteous manner. For example, all church volunteers should be friendly and greet people as part of their role. Inform customers about what to expect and when to expect it. For example, volunteers should make visitors aware of when the church service starts, when it ends, and what they can expect during the service.

Conclude all interactions with customers in a professional and courteous manner. For example, as visitors are leaving the building, the door greeters should thank them for coming.

Demonstrate respect for each other and hold ourselves and each other accountable for appropriate behavior. For example, teams of volunteers should watch out for each other and challenge each other if they see someone not behaving appropriately.

Dress Code

It always helps to communicate what's appropriate and what isn't appropriate to wear when serving in a volunteer capacity. Some churches have very formal dress codes (suits, ties, skirts, jackets) while others are less formal (business casual, jeans). It just depends on the culture and tradition of the church. Regardless, volunteers should know the code.

Chain of Command

Volunteers must understand the church chain of command, not so much to recognize who the "boss" is but to know where to go with issues, concerns, or problems. For instance, if the volunteer found that the restroom was out of hand soap, he would need to know which staff employee or volunteer to go to in order to replenish the supplies. This way, the volunteer doesn't ask the pastor about soap right before he's getting ready to preach to the congregation. A printed organizational chart is also very helpful.

Communications Process

Volunteers need lots of information about events, changes or other things going on with the church, so they should know where to find the information they need. For example, a volunteer should know whom to call if she has to miss her scheduled shift. Or, if volunteer schedules are on the church website, every volunteer should know to go there for that information. Active communication keeps people engaged and makes them feel valued. The trick is to share information before it's asked for.

Volunteer Program

Volunteer orientation is a great time to explain the volunteer program and how it supports the volunteers.

Taking a few minutes to explain how to contact the volunteer office and the services it provides will help volunteers understand who, how, and when to communicate.

Volunteers are one of the church's greatest assets. Making sure they have proper supervision and they receive thorough communication and understand their roles as volunteers can help set the stage for a fulfilling volunteer experience.

Volunteer Job Description

Example: Church Volunteer Job Description

Effective volunteer management involves good communication and coordination of job duties. Like employees, it's important for volunteers to have a clear understanding of what the church expects of them, and they need to have the training and tools to perform tasks. A well-run volunteer program will include a streamlined process to recruit, place, and train volunteers in the role that best matches their personality, interests, and skill sets.

A volunteer job description should have enough details to describe not only jobs but also job hours and where to go to get questions answered.

When writing a church volunteer job description, it's important to answer the following questions: Who? What? Where? When? How? By considering the job tasks, going through a simple process of asking these questions can flush out the necessary details for the job description.

So what does this mean? Who does the volunteer report to? For example, who oversees ushers and who does the volunteer report to?

What tasks is the volunteer responsible for performing? For example, what does the usher do when he/she is on duty? Where does he or she do the job? For instance, where do ushers meet before, during, and after church services and where do they hang their coats or purses while on duty?

When does the volunteer receive the assignment to work? When does the volunteer's shift begin and end? At what time should the volunteer report to duty? For example, what's the usher schedule, and when does the shift begin and end.

How does the volunteer perform job responsibilities? For example, how do ushers dress, how do they communicate with guests, how do they take the offering, etc.

Using the template below, let's now create an example of a church volunteer job description.

Example: Volunteer Job Description

Example Church Volunteer

Job Description

ABC Community Church

Volunteer Title:	Usher
Reports to:	Elder Smith ← WHO
Scheduled Shift:	Sunday 7 a.m. – 11:30 a.m. ← WHEN
Job Location:	Volunteer Room ← WHERE

Job Duties: ←WHAT

- Straighten chairs in auditorium.
- Fill chair pockets with offering envelopes.
- Stack offering baskets.
- Place bulletins in bins by all doors.
- Usher guests to seats.

The process of creating job descriptions is quick and efficient with a few of the right people in the room. Gather a few folks who understand the needs, sit in a room with a laptop, and just go down the list and answer the questions. You'll be surprised at how quickly you can create volunteer role descriptions.

Church volunteers are valuable assets for any ministry, which is why it's vital to provide good systems and processes to support them. Investing some time thinking through and creating detailed job descriptions is one way to show your volunteers you value and support them.

CHAPTER 9

Customer Focus

"Be diligent to know the state of your flocks, And attend to your herds…" Proverbs 27:23

Customer Focus

This chapter is about people. These are fictitious characters that may represent any number of people within a church. Doug may be the first-time visitor who's looking for a church and longing to find the right environment for his family. Ella may be that congregant who shows up for church week after week and is trying to find her place in the body of Christ. Bill may be the volunteer who's committed and shows up for his shift week after week but may need to have periodic interaction with the person who oversees his volunteer role. Or Stacy may be that employee who has faithfully served on the church staff and just needs to know that what she does matters and that she gets the support she needs to do her job, which affects the other three groups: members, visitors, and volunteers.

Teaching biblical principles without care and compassion is futile. The church is starting to recognize the importance of meeting the needs of its congregants, volunteers, and employees within the confines of the vision.

These three vital customer groups make up the church, and without them, there is no church. Congregants fund the church, volunteers do the work of the church, and employees facilitate the process.

What does a customer expect from a church?

An Inviting Facility

Those of us living in the prosperous United States have become accustomed to nice, comfortable facilities. Whether it's a mall, hotel, or grocery store, we have learned to expect clean, orderly, and inviting environments.

It's no different for the church, which is why paying attention to the details is important. For example, when visitors drive into the church parking lot, what do they see? Is there debris in the flowerbeds, or are the bushes and plants neatly trimmed?

When they walk in the church's front door, are the windows cloudy with fingerprints, or are there freshly painted walls and pleasant scents? All of these subtle details affect the first-time experience.

Our church home is very similar to our own home in that those nicks on the wall and stains on the carpet become so familiar to us we have the tendency to overlook them.

But a visitor sees these things immediately when she first walks in the door. You know how it goes; nobody notices when your house is clean, but everybody notices it when it's disorderly and dirty.

Friendly People

When visitors walk through the doors of a church they're searching for something. Very often, these people are at a low point in their lives, and they've come to realize their need for a church experience. Other times, people are searching for the right church home for their family.

Either case, a visitor will assess a church experience by how welcoming and friendly the people are. The challenge with this is some people want to be noticed and identified as visitors and others want to visit without a lot of fanfare, so striking the balance is a challenge and a training opportunity.

Visitors walk into churches every day and quickly assess the experience. Smaller churches can probably identify visitors quickly and have a plan to welcome them. Larger churches don't always have this luxury, so they need to create an environment that's welcoming for everyone who walks through the door.

People who are new to a church want to connect with the church family and need help learning how to establish friendships. Providing an inviting experience and friendly first-time contacts will make people feel welcomed.

What Does the Body Want?

The congregation is the body of the church. Each part of the body has a role to play, and each has its own unique needs. Each of us is on a personal journey, and we all have specific spiritual needs. The congregation's expectations are dependent on the organization's ability to share the mission and vision. When congregants understand where the church is going and buy into the vision, they offer volunteer labor and financial support. However, there are times when members have needs and expectations (sometimes demands) that don't line up with the vision. For example, a young couple with small children will expect the church to offer a great children's program for their kids (which would line up with most church visions).

Another congregant may have an interest in setting up a table in the lobby to sell Girl Scout cookies, which may not line up with the vision. The ability to support those needs that line up with the vision is important, while meeting unreasonable demands is not.

Every church operates by a different guiding mission and vision, which affects its focus and priorities. This means the needs and expectations of congregants may be different from church to church.

The tricky part of overseeing a church body is the responsibility to stay true to the call and vision for the church. This is difficult because congregants sometimes have needs that don't always line up with the vision. When this happens, congregants may decide to look for a church that better meets their needs. These are very difficult situations, but maintaining focus on the mission has to take priority to fulfill God's purpose for the church.

Church Survey Questions

People get involved in the local church to develop relationships, grow spiritually, and participate in the mission of the organization. The members benefit from the opportunities they have, and the church benefits through member financial support and free labor to fulfill its mission. When done well, it's a win-win!

Tensions arise when either party feels as if they have unmet needs. Church leadership can become frustrated from dealing with high maintenance members who seem to ask for more than they contribute, and members can become frustrated when they perceive that the church isn't meeting their core spiritual needs.

The interesting dynamic of the church is that it often avoids conflict because Christians want others to perceive them as nice and kind, which can result in no one addressing or resolving issues. Another interesting dynamic is that the leadership is often unaware of member frustrations. This can sadly result in unresolved issues and member defection. Soliciting feedback is one way to determine the perception of how well the church is meeting member needs.

I discovered that complaints are often a gift and a learning experience. Church leaders need to understand church member perceptions and develop systems to meet their needs as long as their needs fall under the umbrella of the vision and mission of the organization. This is another reason to have a clearly defined and well-known vision and mission statement that helps members understand what the church is trying to achieve.

When developing a church survey, it's important to think about those things that affect the member experience. Ask questions about processes that influence the experience, things like how the church shares its information, how well members understand services, or how well the church meets the spiritual needs of the family.

How Do We Assess the Customer Experience?

Soliciting feedback helps the church learn about the customer perspective and identifies ways to improve the customer experience. Just like any other request for learning what someone thinks, customer opinions can sting, but reflection on honest feedback can shed light on areas that need improvement.

The saying "Sometimes the truth hurts" is a very true and important part of any improvement model. I always told my employees "I can't fix it if I don't know it's broken." My goal in saying this was to help them feel comfortable, sharing the sometimes difficult issues we need to deal with.

Leadership can't make improvements unless they know the issues exist, and the only way to know that is for the person who's experiencing the process to give an honest perspective. For example, if an employee in the children's ministry is checking families in on a computer that's outdated and not functioning properly, it will affect the parent experience. It's important to make sure the employee (customer of the church) has good equipment to take care of the parents (customer of the church).

Congregation Feedback

Church members fund the church operation and are an important customer group.

Looking at how the church meets its members' spiritual, social, and physical needs is important as long as those needs line up with the mission and vision of the church.

For example, if the church learns that a congregant has concerns about how the church communicates with its members, this may be an issue that warrants further investigation and some changes. If another congregant voices concerns about the church not allowing him to use the auditorium for an event that isn't church-related, it's important to communicate with that church member to explain the reasons.

Soliciting feedback from church members helps to identify issues, and it opens lines of communication. There are individuals all around us and as church leaders we need to understand who they are, what they need from the church, and how to make their church experience, whether they're a visitor, congregant, volunteer, or employee, one they will remember and bring their families and friends to experience.

Sample Questions for a Church Survey

ABC Community Church Member Survey	
Please circle the number that corresponds with your level of agreement. **Strongly Disagree = 1 Disagree = 5 Strongly Agree = 10**	
1. Overall, I am satisfied as a member of ABC Church.	1 2 3 4 5 6 7 8 9 10
2. ABC Church cares about its members.	1 2 3 4 5 6 7 8 9 10
3. I receive the information I need regarding church projects and decisions.	1 2 3 4 5 6 7 8 9 10
4. I have a good understanding of the mission and vision of ABC Church.	1 2 3 4 5 6 7 8 9 10
5. ABC Church meets the spiritual needs of its members.	1 2 3 4 5 6 7 8 9 10
6. I understand the process of becoming a church volunteer.	1 2 3 4 5 6 7 8 9 10
7. I feel as if I'm part of a team helping to fulfill the mission of ABC Church.	1 2 3 4 5 6 7 8 9 10
8. ABC Church is welcoming to visitors and new church members.	1 2 3 4 5 6 7 8 9 10
9. I believe our mission and vision drive church decisions.	1 2 3 4 5 6 7 8 9 10
10. I have opportunities for spiritual growth and leadership.	1 2 3 4 5 6 7 8 9 10
11. I believe ABC Church cares about the spiritual development of my family.	1 2 3 4 5 6 7 8 9 10
12. I intend to continue my membership at ABC Church.	1 2 3 4 5 6 7 8 9 10
13. Please tell us one thing ABC Church could do to better achieve its mission.	
Comments	

Adding a rating scale to the survey tool helps to determine the degree of respondents' agreement or disagreement with the question. I like to use a 10-point scale because it creates a more sensitive instrument.

Are Employees Customers?

It may take a paradigm shift to think of employees as a customer group, but they're probably the most important customer group any organization has. Employees facilitate the process of making "church" happen and often with limited resources. This requires a special calling that's unique to church employees. Church leadership should recognize the unique aspects of being a church employee and provide the resources and support to ensure a great employee experience.

Employees are customers of each other (department-to-department). For example, think of how the IT person supports the church secretary. Employees with fulfilled needs are better equipped to take care of the other customers (volunteers, congregants, and visitors) that they serve.

Employee Feedback

Employees are among a church's most valuable assets, and providing a pleasant work environment is important to ensuring that the church takes care of all customer groups.

If employees lack the necessary resources—time, equipment, and training—to do their jobs, they will have a difficult time providing the necessary support to their customers.

ABC Community Church Employee Survey	
Please circle the number that corresponds with your level of agreement. **Strongly Disagree = 1 Disagree = 5 Strongly Agree = 10**	
1. Overall, I am satisfied as an employee of ABC Church.	1 2 3 4 5 6 7 8 9 10
2. My pay is competitive with other places I could work.	1 2 3 4 5 6 7 8 9 10
3. ABC Church cares about its employees.	1 2 3 4 5 6 7 8 9 10
4. ABC Church cares about its customers (employees, volunteers, members).	1 2 3 4 5 6 7 8 9 10
5. I receive the information I need regarding the issues that affect me.	1 2 3 4 5 6 7 8 9 10
6. My supervisor shows appreciation for the work I do.	1 2 3 4 5 6 7 8 9 10
7. My job description accurately reflects what I am asked to do.	1 2 3 4 5 6 7 8 9 10
8. I received the training I need to perform my job duties	1 2 3 4 5 6 7 8 9 10
9. I feel I am part of a team helping to fulfill the mission of ABC Church.	1 2 3 4 5 6 7 8 9 10
10. Managers confront employees who are weak in customer service.	1 2 3 4 5 6 7 8 9 10
11. I have the ability to meet or exceed the needs of my customers.	1 2 3 4 5 6 7 8 9 10
12. I feel secure in having a job at ABC Church as long as I perform well.	1 2 3 4 5 6 7 8 9 10
13. I believe our mission and vision drive the decisions that are made.	1 2 3 4 5 6 7 8 9 10
14. I am provided opportunities for job growth and development.	1 2 3 4 5 6 7 8 9 10
15. My supervisor helps me understand the strategic goals for ABC Church.	1 2 3 4 5 6 7 8 9 10
16. I intend to continue my employment at ABC Church.	1 2 3 4 5 6 7 8 9 10
13. Please tell us one thing ABC Church could do to better achieve its mission.	
Comments	

Volunteer Feedback

Volunteers are the labor engine of a church and having a good understanding of how the church meets their needs is important to keeping them engaged and committed to the church and their job responsibilities. Volunteer feedback provides insight into the volunteer experience and allows the ministry to learn how to improve the process of volunteer recruitment, placement, training, and job assignments.

Volunteer Survey

Volunteers give their time because they care about the organization and have a passion for its mission and vision. Keeping volunteers engaged ensures maintaining a long-term relationship, and one way to engage them is to provide an opportunity to offer feedback to the organization.

This makes it important to create a system that facilitates two-way communication between the organization and its volunteers. This two-way communication is a great way to improve how the organization does what it does, by taking advantage of the volunteers' collective experiences and perspectives.

Volunteers are often the front-line support and experience the process of delivering a service or product and can very often articulate what works and what needs improvement in the operational process. Successful organizations understand the value of listening to their customer feedback. In the nonprofit world, one of the main customer groups is the volunteers.

Create a Feedback Process

Understanding the volunteer experience can help support volunteers as does incorporating a structured feedback process into the volunteer management program. Structure the feedback process in such a way that there are predictable times to ask volunteers about their experience. This kind of structure helps to ensure supervisors identify issues quickly and volunteers become comfortable with sharing personal perspectives.

Volunteers can be the biggest advocates for the organization, and taking advantage of their perspective provides valuable information to use to improve the volunteer experience as well as the services the organization provides.

4 Opportunities to Solicit Volunteer Feedback

1. Baseline Feedback

If your organization has never solicited feedback from your volunteers, the first step is to gather some baseline data by looking at the global experience of the volunteer. You do this to help identify any improvement opportunities to use to develop and enhance the volunteer program.

The advantage in asking for this kind of feedback is that the volunteers will willingly provide all the information needed to put together an improvement plan that can help take the volunteer program to the next level. This kind of feedback gives you an idea about how the volunteer program is supporting the volunteers and what the program can do logistically to improve the volunteer experience.

2. Annual Surveys

Gather the baseline data, share it with the leadership, and put plans into action to address any suggestions or concerns. Once implemented, it's time to resurvey the volunteers and try to learn whether the improvements addressed the issues the volunteers identified.

One way to do this is to send the survey out monthly to smaller groups of volunteer so that you begin collecting monthly data. This approach can help to identify issues on a monthly basis rather than waiting for the annual survey.

To do this, simply take your volunteer database and sort it into 12 different groupings. The groupings can be alphabetical, by volunteer area, or just random. Any way is fine as long as you keep track of who received a survey, and when they received it, so you don't accidently send the same person a survey month after month.

3. After Special Events

Planning and facilitating big events takes a lot of work, great organization, and loads of logistical detail. Volunteers who help with events always have a great perspective for what worked and what things could use improvement.

They see things from two perspectives. The first is their own experience as a volunteer. Things like how well the communication process was, did the training prepare them well for their volunteer role, did they have everything they needed to perform their job tasks, etc.

The second perspective is how they met the needs of the people they served. Volunteers are the first point of contact and hear direct responses whether it's gratitude or dissatisfaction about something.

Volunteers get exposure to information the organization needs to know. Following up with volunteers after a big event can provide information to use to improve the event and the people it serves.

4. Small Group Meetings

Sometimes leaders host meetings with a smaller group of volunteers for perhaps special training, information sharing, or even event planning. When these types of meetings take place, it's always good to solicit volunteer input. Like employees, volunteers are closest to the processes and have a great perspective on how to improve operational processes, and it's in these intimate settings that structured conversation can lead to great insights.

Sample Volunteer Survey

ABC Community Church Volunteer Survey	
Please circle the number that corresponds with your level of agreement. **Strongly Disagree = 1 Disagree = 5 Strongly Agree = 10**	
1. Overall, I am satisfied as a volunteer of ABC Church.	1 2 3 4 5 6 7 8 9 10
2. ABC Church cares about its volunteers.	1 2 3 4 5 6 7 8 9 10
3. I receive the information I need regarding my volunteer role.	1 2 3 4 5 6 7 8 9 10
4. My volunteer supervisor shows appreciation for the work I do.	1 2 3 4 5 6 7 8 9 10
5. My volunteer job description accurately reflects what I am asked to do.	1 2 3 4 5 6 7 8 9 10
6. I have received the training I need to perform my volunteer job duties.	1 2 3 4 5 6 7 8 9 10
7. I feel I am part of a team helping to fulfill the mission of ABC Church.	1 2 3 4 5 6 7 8 9 10
8. Managers confront volunteers who are weak in customer service.	1 2 3 4 5 6 7 8 9 10
9. I believe our mission and vision drive church decisions.	1 2 3 4 5 6 7 8 9 10
10. I am provided opportunities to grow in my volunteer role.	1 2 3 4 5 6 7 8 9 10
11. My volunteer supervisor helps me understand the mission of ABC Church.	1 2 3 4 5 6 7 8 9 10
12. I intend to continue volunteering at ABC Church.	1 2 3 4 5 6 7 8 9 10
13. Please tell us one thing ABC Church could do to better achieve its mission.	
Comments	

Other considerations when surveying customer groups:

- Keep the survey as short as possible and limit the questions to 15 or fewer. The longer the survey the lower the response rate.

- Make sure the scale is clear so there are no accidental ratings. If someone accidentally rates all questions with a 1 and means to rate a 10, your data will be skewed.
- Take some time to conduct a focus group with a select group to expand on responses.
- Add a comment section with adequate writing space. You will often learn more from the comments than the scores.
- Make the survey process as easy as possible by providing easy and quick access to the tool and response locations.
- Add a section for demographic information so you can determine if age, gender, etc. contributes to certain perceptions.
- Don't take negative comments personally. It's not about you; it's about the process. Consider them a gift of learning what to improve.
- Don't spend the time or energy asking for feedback unless you're committed to developing a plan to address identified issues.

This can be an expensive project if you hire a company to administer a survey. If you don't have the resources for that, there are many inexpensive or free tools you can use. One is in Google Docs, and it's quick, efficient, and FREE! All you have to do is email it to members, and the results come back in an easy-to-read report.

Take what you learn, develop an improvement plan, and share it with the group surveyed to show your commitment to making things better!

CHAPTER 10

Public Relations

Public Relations

Public relations is about how the community it serves perceives the organization. But do churches really need public relations? Should they care about how others view them? The answer is yes because the church represents Christ, and the church body has a responsibility to represent Christ with excellence and maintain a positive public image.

Developing a public relations strategy is instrumental to influencing the church's public image and perception. A good strategy can help build rapport with congregants, employees, and the public. The goal would be for the ministry to have a good reputation within the community. A well-thought-out strategy is useful as part of a comprehensive plan and provides a roadmap for a public response during times of crisis.

Creating an Effective Public Relations Strategy

Discovery

Discovery is a process an organization goes through to understand what their church is, who it serves, and who it interacts with in the community. This process involves very specific strategies and research.

For instance, a church supported homeless shelter may have a vision to "provide shelter to those who have temporarily lost the ability to provide for themselves." This statement helps an organization understand who they are, what their mission is, and who they serve.

The ministry will then try to identify who in the community they interact with. In the case of a homeless shelter, it may be residents or businesses within the neighborhood they serve. The church should have a goal to create a positive relationship with everyone it interacts with. This is important because, in the case of a homeless shelter, a positive relationship can possibly increase funding, identify volunteer labor, or foster collaboration for joint community projects.

Public Relations Plan

Developing the PR plan is very similar to establishing church goals and is part of a strategic planning process. Focus PR goals and objectives on communicating what you learned in the discovery phase. Have a well-thought-out communication plan for congregants, employees, the public, and those who interact with the organization. For instance, how does the ministry make the public aware of the homeless shelter?

Another part of the plan is developing strategy for how the organization can be both active and reactive.

The plan is active by educating the public on the services the church provides as well as maintaining a positive public image. The plan is reactive in how the ministry plans to respond to unplanned or unforeseen events. Having a written strategy is the key to facilitating a positive response.

An important part of the plan is to identify the person who speaks on behalf of the organization, the message, as well as the tone of the message. It takes specialized training for someone to field questions from the media, so having a person with the right skill set and gift is critical.

Public Relations Policy

PR policy should have instructions how to communicate or respond to any number of situations. This includes communicating with employees or the news media or an announcement as part of an advertising campaign. For example, identifying what and how to communicate information about a community outreach event is an important part of the policy creation.

Plan Implementation

Implementing the plan according to policy requires budgeting, scheduling, and a process to roll out the plan. Budgeting and timing of implementation is critical to the result. For example, printed material about a church-sponsored event or community outreach may be a budget line item.

Evaluation

It's important to evaluate the performance of how well the plan is working, and having SMART goals can provide measures for tracking success over time. Using the PDCA model of quality improvement can also help facilitate a consistent process.

A good PR strategy can help build relationships with congregants, donors, employees, and the public. Having a reputation for positive things, such as giving back to the community, being a welcoming place to worship, or being supportive of other social needs can do more to acquire new members than any other form of advertising. People like to connect with a church that's doing the work of the Kingdom!

CHAPTER 11

Getting the Word Out

How do people know what we do?

Church Marketing (not a four-letter word!)

Churches do a lot of great things, but very often people don't even know about it. This is why churches need to think about how to make people aware of what they do. The digital age has provided many low cost tools that can help get the word out. The challenge becomes getting up to speed on the latest technologies and using them as communication tools.

Internet Presence

An Internet presence for the church is critical in this digital age. Kids have grown up on the Internet and use it to research and seek out information. Like any other organization, churches must have an Internet presence that appeals to this generation. You may never get them in the door if they base their perception of the church on Internet research that's less than positive. I've heard people more than once say they visited a church because of how its website looked!

Online Directories

You should list the church on as many free online directories as you can. Here are a few you can set up accounts with. Make sure your information is accurate. Many of these sites pull information from various sources, and they don't verify the information for you. You need to check it out and make sure the information is accurate. Here are a few of the most common directories you might want to make sure has a listing for your church.

Moz—moz.com/local

Yelp—yelp.com

Yellow Pages—yp.com

Google Places—google.com/local/business

Bing Places—bingplaces.com

Website

When my family and I moved, I found my current church by doing an Internet search for churches. And I decided to visit because the website was professional, informative, and easy to use. People will judge churches by how their website looks. Its website represents the organization's culture and style. Take the time to create a site that's current, informative, and easy to use.

If you don't have a website, do a little research and check out the sites of other churches. Set your bar high and dare to look at the website of the large church down the street. It probably has more resources than you, so don't feel discouraged by what you see. Rather, get some ideas for creating your own site.

If you have a website built 10 years ago, it may be time to give it a facelift. The technology has changed a lot, and the look and feel of websites is constantly evolving. Try to stay current since your website may be the tool that either brings visitors to your church or sends them away.

Blog

Blogging is a form of giving back and engages others in topical conversations. Creating a church blog is a great way to interact with the congregation and share biblical concepts every day of the week. For example, writing a blog post on Monday about the Sunday sermon that goes deeper into the topic can provide supplemental teaching for congregants.

Social Media

Ten years ago, no one heard of Facebook or Twitter.

Communicating with church members was typically through email or printed copy with an occasional phone call.

Big church events sometimes warranted a press release to share information to those outside the organization.

Churches are often laggards when it comes to technology trends but are now learning to take advantage of available social technologies to improve communications with their members. According to a recent Barna study, the number of pastors and churches who engage in social media has increased significantly in the past couple of years.

The study suggests that 21 percent of American pastors now use Twitter, which is up from 14 percent in 2011. Likewise, 70 percent of churches are now using Facebook and 22 percent of pastors now have a personal blog. There are some differences with size of church, annual contributions, and age of pastors, but more churches are now realizing the benefits of social communications.

5 Tips for Using Social Media

1. Develop a Church Social Media Strategy

The use of social technologies should be part of every organization's strategic plan, and incorporating social media into church goals should be part of that strategy. Take some time and research what works in other organizations and then brainstorm ways to use social tools to communicate with members and your community.

2. Set Goals for Church Social Media

Setting goals, and holding employees accountable for achieving goals, is how to get work done. Developing specific goals and targets for social media is part of that process. Think about with whom (target audience), what (message), and how (process) the church wants to communicate and establish the processes to ensure that it's consistent.

3. Assign Responsibility

Once established, a social communication plan must have someone who's responsible for the work. Social tools are only as effective as the frequency of use. Don't allow it to turn into one of those things that someone does only after finishing all other competing responsibilities. Assign the task to someone and require accountability!

4. Solicit Feedback

Talk to church members and have them help identify ways to use social tools to better communicate with both inside and outside of the church. Conduct a focus group and try to gain new ideas from your employees, volunteers, and members.

5. Write Church Social Media Policy

Establishing a process for social communication is important to ensure consistency and quality of content. Once created, write the policy and train employees and volunteers (if applicable) on the newly established internal boundaries and requirements. No one knows what new technologies will be available 10 years from now, but churches and nonprofit organizations should take advantage of the many tools that are available now to improve church communications and spread the message!

This list of social tools should give you a good starting point:

Facebook

Facebook is a social phenomenon used by millions of people worldwide to connect to each other. Every generation now looks at Facebook, and churches should capture the moment to interact with its congregants. For instance, a church can create a Facebook page and share information about specific outreach or ministry events.

Twitter

Twitter is a 140-character message sent to cell phones, making it quick and timely and is a great way to keep in touch with congregants.

For example, a youth pastor can tweet a daily scripture to youth, or the volunteer office can tweet a call for volunteers.

Instagram

Instagram is a great tool for sharing pictures. Use this tool to share pictures of kids in children's church, highlights of church events, or participation in church programs.

Pinterest

Pinterest is another picture-sharing site. Use Pinterest to share helpful articles and information about church. You can create boards to share information. For example, pin a blog post highlighting your vacation Bible school with pictures of the kids participating.

YouTube

The YouTube generation is strong and growing. This new phenomenon in communication has rewritten the rules for marketing, advertising, and public awareness. The sight and sound generation has redefined how we communicate, and video is the tool of choice. YouTube has some interesting statistics:

- YouTube has more than 1 billion users
- Every day people watch hundreds of millions of hours on YouTube and generate billions of views
- People upload 300 hours of video to YouTube every minute.
- Half of YouTube views are on mobile devices.

These statistics are staggering and the numbers grow every day. With the video capabilities on most phones, shooting a video and posting it to YouTube is quick, easy, and free!

So why would a church want to use this phenomenal tool? Or the better question might be why wouldn't a ministry take advantage of YouTube?

Ways to use YouTube videos in church PR strategy:

Senior Pastor Introductions

A YouTube video is a great way for visitors to get to know the senior pastor and staff members. The senior pastor can share the vision and plans for the church.

YouTube is only one video tool that can incorporate into a church website to gain exposure and credibility for the church. This kind of strategy can help engage potential visitors in what the ministry is doing.

Volunteer/Employee Recruitment

Churches can use YouTube to recruit employees. Using video of current employees to describe the value in working for a ministry can help spark interest in potential job candidates.

Ministry Program Description

Video is a quick and effective way to describe the benefits of participating in a church program. Whether it's helping with the children's ministry or serving the seniors of the church, a video can help demonstrate the benefits of participating. This is especially helpful when launching new ministries.

Philanthropic Support

Many churches rally around a cause, and a video describing the support for a philanthropic effort can help solicit donations for the same cause. For instance, if a church operates a food bank, it could create a video showing the lives it affects and the importance of financial support.

Ministry Advertisements

YouTube is also a great avenue to show off ministries within the church.

The same promotional video that historically would have run on television can now run on the Internet, and it's a much less expensive way to get the word out. For example, a video showing the great things the youth program does could create an interest in the program.

People go to the Internet to find information, and a video description of a service or ministry offered at your church is an excellent way to get the promotion in front of many eyes. And the great thing about YouTube videos is they don't have to look professionally done, and you can create them for minimal cost.

As we've seen, there are many technologies and tools you can use to get the word out. Don't get overwhelmed, start with one, master it, and expand to other tools. The church does great work and taking advantage of all the new technologies today is an exciting way to keep the public informed of what the church is doing.

CHAPTER 12

Emergency Planning

"By faith Noah, being divinely warned of things not yet seen, moved with godly fear, prepared an ark for the saving of his household, by which he condemned the world and became heir of the righteousness which is according to faith."
Hebrews 11:7

Church Emergency Planning

The extreme weather patterns and escalated violence in public places remind us that now is a good time to stop and think about how to plan, prepare, and be ready to respond in the event of an emergency or disaster.

A disaster can be defined as a natural disaster (flood, hurricane, tornado, and earthquake), an act of terrorism, (think 9/11) or an armed intruder (Charleston Church Shooting). Each of these occurrences has its own unique issues, but there are some common things you can and should do to prepare.

Most emergencies or disasters happen without much warning.

Even those with some warning don't allow enough time to come up with an emergency management plan.

So what is an emergency management plan?

It's a written document that answers the questions of **who, what, where, when,** and **how** to get the church back up and running following a disaster or emergency. An emergency management plan can have as much detail as you like or be as simple as thinking through some basic logistical first steps.

Obviously, the more detailed your plan is, the less "thinking" you need to do at a time when there's chaos and many logistical challenges. Imagine your church running without computer systems, communication systems, employee support, or a functioning facility. Thinking through the "what if" helps prepare.

Emergency planning requires a team made up of representatives from senior leadership, information technology, facilities management, and support employees. This team is responsible for thinking through all of the logistical "what if" questions. For example,

- What is the communication process in an emergency?
- Who do we communicate with and in what order?
- Who is the spokesperson for media questions?
- Where is the command center if the current campus is not available?
- How do we manage without a computer network?
- Did the responsible person back up the network files?
- How can we get hardware quickly?
- How do we communicate without a phone system?
- How do we share information with the congregation, volunteers, and employees?
- Where should we have temporary church services?

Once you have a plan in place, it's important to go through a fictitious "what if" scenario to test your plan. Many organizations hold what they call disaster drills to test their plans and use the exercise to learn how to improve the plan. It's amazing how different things look when you go through the process of implementing recovery steps. I have worked with teams who have gone through these drills and cannot emphasize how valuable the experience is and well worth the time investment.

So what are some things you should think about in the time of crisis or disaster? There are typically three phases of any disaster or emergency, first response, clean-up, and recovery

First Response

In the first response phase, the initial need is to ensure the safety and security of the facility and provide immediate help to possible victims. This can include life-sustaining efforts, first aid, food, water, and basic living essentials. This phase also includes preparing to handle any media inquiries that would require having an articulate scripted spokesperson prepared to represent the ministry.

Clean-up Phase

This includes cleaning up any damage and getting the facility prepared for employees, volunteers, and members to reenter. In the case of an armed intruder, give a lot of thought on how to mentally and spiritually prepare church members to return to the campus. This is also the phase where grief counseling is perhaps a good idea.

Recovery Phase

The final recovery phase is getting the facility back in order and ready to reopen for church services. Depending on the emergency or disaster, this may take a few days, weeks, or months. In the case of a long-term recovery process, it's critical to have a designated place to have church services as well as a command center where a leadership team can help facilitate the recovery process.

This includes communicating with members, volunteers, employees, and the general public.

An Emergency Management Plan Manual should include:

- ✓ Well-thought-out steps of action for each of the three phases of recovery. (This is where you will identify the who, what, where, when, and how.)
- ✓ Emergency contact information for employees, volunteers, key members, and supply vendors
- ✓ Information system requirements for hardware, software, and business data backup files
- ✓ Telephone system layout
- ✓ Diagrams of building layout
- ✓ IT network diagram
- ✓ A call tree of the leadership team, essentially the chain of command (who gets notified first and who notifies whom)
- ✓ Once completed, the manual should be one of several items placed in an emergency management box. Keep this box at a location away from the church campus.
- ✓ Contents of the emergency management box should include:
- ✓ Emergency management plan manual
- ✓ Employee manual
- ✓ Copies of insurance documents and policies
- ✓ Hard drive with computer software
- ✓ Backup files on all key business data
- ✓ Employee contact information
- ✓ Key member and vendor contact information
- ✓ Name tags for employees in case they need identification to cross into restricted areas

- ✓ Basic office supplies (paper, pens, tape, stapler, etc.)

Update the box every six months to keep contents and contact information current. Here are two websites that are useful in helping you prepare your organization for unexpected emergencies: ready.gov and fema.gov.

There will always be unpredictable aspects to any disaster, but a little upfront planning can take a chaotic emergency and turn it into a smooth-running recovery process.

CHAPTER 13

Event Planning

"And they continued steadfastly in the apostles' doctrine and fellowship, in the breaking of bread, and in prayers."
Acts 2:42

Event Planning

Events and churches have long gone hand-in-hand because church families enjoy time together and often seek out ways to gather as a group. So whether it's the annual children's vacation Bible school, church picnic, or a church anniversary celebration, having a template for event planning is crucial to facilitating great church events.

Most events entail the same elements that will fit in an event template, and the planning simply requires thinking through the details of each element. After you complete it, you can streamline the event planning so it's efficient and fun!

10 Elements of Planning a Church Event

1. Event Goal

It's always helpful to understand what the goal of an event is. Questions you need to ask:

- Is this event to provide fellowship?
- Is it community outreach?

- Is it a fundraiser to raise money for a cause?

Depending on the event's goal, the planning can vary. Make sure your planning team understands the why behind the event.

2. Event Budget

Planning for any event should always begin with a budget. Understanding how much money is available to support the event is critical to the planning process. You must determine whether there will be any money raised at the event or whether it's strictly an opportunity to give back to the congregation or community.

An event budget should include things like marketing materials, decorations, food, entertainment, equipment rental, and supplies. Enter each of these line items when putting together an event budget.

3. Church Event Theme

Every event should have an identified theme that helps determine all other supporting aspects. A theme helps to create the atmosphere and to stand out throughout the event. For instance, a Mexican theme dictates the kind of food, decorations, music, and atmosphere.

4. Church Event Marketing

Attendance for events is only as high as the church's ability to get the word out or to advertise the event. Create a marketing plan to ensure people are aware of the event and excited about it.

Depending on whether the event is solely for the church or whether it's open to the community dictates the kind of marketing or advertising. It varies as something as simple as posting the event on the church website, in the church bulletin, and weekly announcements to as complex as printed brochures or advertisements on local radio or television. Regardless, taking the time to think through who the target audience is and how to get the word out is an important part of successful event planning.

5. Event Activities

Activities are the fun part of every event and provide things for guests to do. So whether it's planning the games for the church picnic or creating questions for a trivia night, the activity planning should include all details of the activities such as supplies, instructions for playing games, prizes (and how they're awarded), etc. The more detail ahead of time, the fewer "hiccups" there will be on the big day.

6. Food Planning

The food is often the highlight of any event so taking the time to plan and prepare tasty food can help create a memorable experience for guests. So whether the event has a caterer or a group of church volunteers prepares the food, planning the details is imperative. The menu should support the theme and planning for adequate paper goods and food is what ensures a great food experience!

7. Event Setup and Teardown

When I attend big community fairs or art shows, I always think about the invisible army that provides electric power, sets up tents, tables, signage, trashcans, etc. And then the group that shows up after the fact to take it all down and clean up the mess. This is potentially the most important job in facilitating a big event. A well-organized setup and teardown plan can eliminate last-minute chaos and stress for event organizers.

8. Event Decorating

Fun decorations help create atmosphere and are a picturesque way to reinforce an event theme, so have a creative team that can dress up the event. This requires some creative thought and skill at hanging, laying out, or designing decorations. These little added touches can take a mediocre event and turn it into something to remember.

9. Job Duties

Events require people to pull them off so have someone assigned to identify jobs and assign people to those jobs. It also entails creating a chain-of-command and identifying leadership over each area. The larger the event the greater the chain-of-command becomes and the more it needs volunteer help. Regardless of the size of the event, volunteers will need a detailed job description and training to successfully fulfill their job assignments.

10. Organizational Chart

I am a visual person so I like to work with organizational charts because they clearly show who has responsibility for what and what the pecking order is. Chain-of-command is less about who is on the top rung as it is who can make decisions and help facilitate a smooth process.

Here's an example of an event organizational chart:

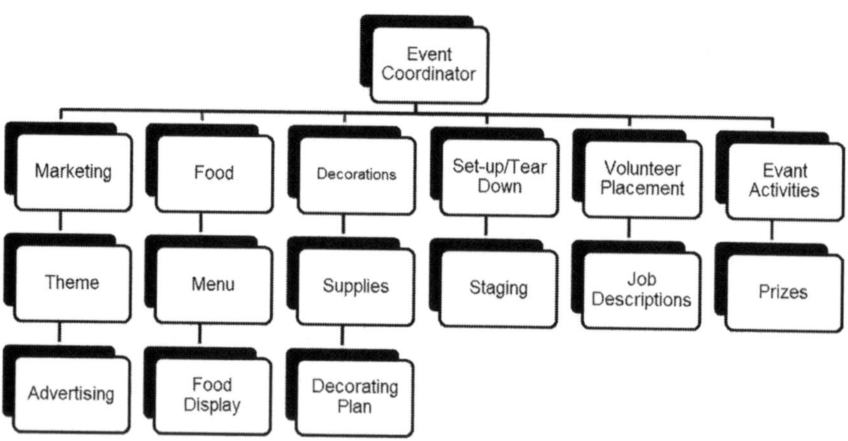

Church events are a lot of fun and can provide great fellowship for a congregation and community. Having a structured church event planning process can help streamline the planning and ensure that no detail gets forgotten.

Debriefing After an Event

Most ministries are really good at planning, gathering volunteers, and hosting church-sponsored events. There are always things to learn when facilitating a church event and taking those valuable tidbits of information and using them to improve the next event will help to improve your events.

Debriefing from a big event captures the moment and takes advantage of the combined knowledge and experience of everyone involved. When those involved in the event have the opportunity to give feedback that's incorporated into future church event planning, events continually improve.

6 Reasons to Debrief From a Church Event

1. Lessons Learned

Planning a big church event is similar to building an engine. The planning builds the parts, organizes them, and puts them all together, and then on the day of the event, you simply turn on the engine and watch it operate. Through this process, there are inevitable things that go on behind the scenes you need to manage and take note of so you can provide valuable information for event organizers.

Lessons learned include capturing fresh information by asking the questions, "what worked" that we should continue to do and "what are the opportunities for improvement' that we can note and consider for the next event.

2. Celebrate Success

Whether the event had a few hiccups or ran smoothly, there's always a reason to celebrate and thank those who helped to make it happen. Taking time in a debrief session to acknowledge the hard work and the outcome keeps employees and volunteers motivated and engaged.

3. Budget Review

Every event should have a budget that includes every aspect of the event. Things like marketing, decorations, food, entertainment, miscellaneous supplies, event admission fees, staff hours are just some of the things to consider when putting together an event budget.

It's vital to review how well the event met budget and look at some of the expenditures you could possibly cut the next time or perhaps add at the next event. Keeping a church event budget at a break-even point is important to ensure compliance with the overall church budget. Most church events aren't to make money, but events should at least pay for themselves. Managing the event budget helps to achieve that goal.

4. Evaluate Volunteer Leaders

A debriefing session is a good time to review all of the volunteer leaders and evaluate their effectiveness in overseeing a process or a team of volunteers. Effective volunteer management uses events as an opportunity to observe volunteers and make note of those with strong leadership abilities as well as identifying those who may need additional mentoring or training.

5. Evaluate Volunteer Training

It doesn't matter how big or small an event is; training is critical to its success, and developing a training program helps to ensure that volunteers understand the goal of the event and how what they do supports that goal. They also need to know practical steps for performing their duties. This may be as simple as showing them how to collect admission tickets to as complicated as procedures for handling cash. Regardless, a debrief session should look at how well the training worked and how consistent volunteers were in following training procedures.

6. Gather Volunteer Feedback

Since volunteers operate most church events, it's a necessity to gather feedback from the volunteers.

Similar to employees, they're the ones who are doing the work, are the closest to the process and the customers, and if allowed, they can share valuable information to improve the event. For example, a church I used to work with does a huge (6000+ kids) summer camp every year that required more than 1000 volunteers to pull it off.

Every year (17+ years now), we asked the volunteers what worked and what needed improvement. The growth and success of this event linked to volunteers offering ideas and suggestions.

Planning a church-sponsored event can be a fun way to create a fellowship environment for congregants or to provide an evangelistic opportunity to expose visitors to the church. Regardless, church events take time and resources, and debriefing from the event is one way to ensure everyone used those resources appropriately, and they met the event's objective.

CHAPTER 14

ECFA

Does Your Church Have the ECFA (Evangelical Council for Financial Accountability) Seal?

Church leaders answer their call to lead a congregation and may have a lot of training in theology and biblical principles. But many of these leaders do not have basic business training required to manage church resources, people, time, and money. This results in churches needing help with developing systems and processes not only to support the fulfillment of its mission but also to ensure responsible stewardship of the resources God supplies.

We have all heard the disheartening stories of churches that fell victim to embezzlement, have gotten into trouble for not complying with state or federal tax laws, or churches that may have had financial problems. More often than not, these types of issues arise more out of ignorance (not knowing the proper way to manage resources) rather than intentional neglect. The good news is there are organizations available to help the local church with financial management practices to ensure there are the necessary resources to fulfill its mission.

The Evangelical Council for Financial Accountability (ECFA) dedicates itself to helping Christian organizations earn the public trust by adherence to their Seven Standards of Responsible Stewardship. These standards focus on doctrinal issues, board governance, financial oversight, transparency, use of resources and compliance with laws, and stewardship of charitable gifts. Developed through biblical principles, these standards provide support and direction for Christian nonprofit organizations.

ECFA's Seven Standards of Responsible Stewardship

Standard 1 - Doctrinal Issues—Every organization shall subscribe to a written statement of faith clearly affirming a commitment to the evangelical Christian faith or shall otherwise demonstrate such commitment, and shall operate in accordance with biblical truths and practices.

Standard 2 - Governance—Every organization shall be governed by a responsible board of not less than five individuals, a majority of whom shall be independent, who shall meet at least semiannually to establish policy and review its accomplishments.

Standard 3 - Financial Oversight—Every organization shall prepare complete and accurate financial statements. The board or a committee consisting of a majority of independent members shall approve the engagement of an independent certified public accountant, review the annual financial statements, and maintain appropriate communication with the independent certified public accountant. The board shall be apprised of any material weaknesses in internal control or other significant risks.

Standard 4 - Use of Resources and Compliance with Laws—Every organization shall exercise the appropriate management and controls necessary to provide reasonable assurance that all of the organization's operations are carried out and resources are used in a responsible manner and in conformity with applicable laws and regulations, such conformity taking into account biblical mandates.

Standard 5 - Transparency—Every organization shall provide a copy of its current financial statements upon written request and shall provide other disclosures as the law may require. The financial statements required to comply with Standard 3 must be disclosed under this standard. An organization must provide a report, upon written request, including financial information on any specific project for which it has sought or is seeking gifts.

Standard 6 - Compensation-Setting and Related-Party Transactions—Every organization shall set compensation of its top leader and address related-party transactions in a manner that demonstrates integrity and propriety in conformity with ECFA's Policy for Excellence in Compensation-Setting and Related-Party Transactions.

Standard 7 - Stewardship of Charitable Gifts

7.1 **Truthfulness in Communications**. In securing charitable gifts, all representations of fact, descriptions of the financial condition of the organization, or narratives about events must be current, complete, and accurate. References to past activities or events must be appropriately dated. There must be no material omissions or exaggerations of fact, use of misleading photographs, or any other communication which would tend to create a false impression or misunderstanding.

7.2 **Giver Expectations and Intent**. Statements made about the use of gifts by an organization in its charitable gift appeals must be honored. A giver's intent relates both to what was communicated in the appeal and to any instructions accompanying the gift, if accepted by the organization. Appeals for charitable gifts must not create unrealistic expectations of what a gift will actually accomplish.

7.3 **Charitable Gift Communication**. Every organization shall provide givers appropriate and timely gift acknowledgments.

> **7.4 Acting in the Best Interest of Givers.** When dealing with persons regarding commitments on major gifts, an organization's representatives must seek to guide and advise givers to adequately consider their broad interests. An organization must make every effort to avoid knowingly accepting a gift from, or entering into a contract with, a giver that would place a hardship on the giver or place the giver's future well-being in jeopardy.
>
> **7.5 Percentage Compensation for Securing Charitable Gifts.** An organization may not base compensation of outside stewardship resource consultants or its own staff directly or indirectly on a percentage of charitable contributions raised.

Similar to the Better Business Bureau for Businesses, ECFA requires compliance with these standards that demonstrate responsible management of resources. And, through accreditation assures members and the public that donations are managed appropriately.

When I worked in healthcare, we went through the Joint Commission accreditation process every three years. If you're not familiar with the Joint Commission, this accreditation process ensures that hospitals, and similar organizations, provide safe and quality clinical care.

The process reviews policies and procedures that ensure that day-to-day practices line up with what the organization puts in writing as standard protocol. These protocols make sure the hospital does what it says to provide good patient care.

Hospitals that don't spend the time or energy to go through the Joint Commission accreditation process have a disadvantage of not policing their management and clinical practices, which can ultimately affect the quality of clinical care. Knowing what I know, I would not go to a hospital that does not have Joint Commission accreditation because there's no objective oversight process for ensuring quality care.

In the same way, having ECFA accreditation for your church, or other Christian nonprofit, assures donors the organization has an effective governance and management process to guarantee responsible stewardship of church funds. Taking the time and energy to achieve accreditation is an excellent way to earn the public trust and confidence.

The accreditation process requires some work, but committing the time and resources to fulfilling the requirements is well worth the public trust gained by knowing the church properly manages donor resources. In addition, placing the ECFA seal on your website provides your members and donors confidence in giving.

Whether your church is just starting out or has for a long history, you might want to consider ECFA accreditation. Your donors will be glad you did!

CHAPTER 15

Spiritual Warfare

"If you faint in the day of adversity, Your strength is small."
Proverbs 24:10

Spiritual Warfare

I worked in corporate America for many years before God called me to use my business skills to help the local church, and I remember the very real challenges of being a Christian in a secular environment. I remember experiencing spiritual warfare and resistance, but I felt that was just what comes with being a Christian.

When I first went to work for my church, I met with our senior pastor, and he warned me about how difficult it can be to work for a church because of the sometimes intense spiritual resistance. I remember saying that Christians out in the world deal with spiritual warfare all the time, and I declared I was ready for it.

He said it's a little different when you work for a church. A couple of months later, when I was meeting with the pastor, I confessed he was right. I had noticed it was different; the spiritual resistance was a little more intense.

During the first couple of months working on a church staff, I was mentally bombarded with what I now know was the enemy shooting "fiery" darts at my mind. I continued to keep reading God's Word and learned to identify and resist the attacks. I also recognized that the entire staff dealt with the same thing and that it was our responsibility as leaders to help the employees cope with the spiritual side of working for a ministry.

I soon recognized whenever there were normal office setting issues with the staff the problem seemed a little exaggerated. I came to realize the issues were consistent with any environment that has employees, but the spiritual component made them feel bigger than they were. Normal dealings that pertain to things like communication, team interaction, and team dynamics were most susceptible to attack. I don't think it's a surprise to any Christian that the enemy hates those of us called to help the cause of Christianity, and he's working overtime to discourage and hinder our effectiveness.

Taking the time to teach church employees these concepts and help them to recognize spiritual dynamics and learn how to respond appropriately can help disarm the enemy and keep employees focused on their natural responsibilities. I don't like to over-spiritualize things because there's way too much of that in the world, but I do think it's important to recognize and address those things that hinder the church's progress.

"10 Finally, my brethren, be strong in the Lord and in the power of His might. 11 Put on the whole armor of God, that you may be able to stand against the wiles of the devil. 12 For we do not wrestle against flesh and blood, but against principalities, against powers, against the rulers of the darkness of this age, against spiritual hosts of wickedness in the heavenly places. 13 Therefore take up the whole armor of God that you may be able to withstand in the evil day, and having done all, to stand. 14 Stand therefore, having girded your waist with truth, having put on the breastplate of righteousness, 15 and having shod your feet with the preparation of the gospel of peace; 16 above all, taking the shield of faith with which you will be able to quench all the fiery darts of the wicked one." Ephesians 6:10-16

Strategy

I've counseled in countless situations when an employee was dealing with difficulties and tried to talk the person through the spiritual side of the situation. The same way God cares about every detail of our lives, the enemy loves to disrupt even the slightest of things to get us off track, slow us down, and hinder our progress. For this reason, employees must learn to identify things for what they are and learn to cope and move forward.

One of the best ways to do this is to call a spade a spade. Most Christians can recognize spiritual oppression after they've gone through it, but it's very difficult to see it in the heat of a battle. This is why it's good to have other Christians help. Church staff should know of these difficult aspects of working for a ministry and have the tools and support to resist the enemy.

Providing staff with designated times to meet and discuss the spiritual side of ministry can open the door for meaningful conversations that help keep things in perspective. We set aside time for project planning, so why not invest needed time into the spiritual warfare side of ministry?

CHAPTER 16

Church Growth

Church Growth

Growing a church takes great vision, faithful congregants, discipleship programs, and resources to do all of the above. Growing churches realize that growth comes from a great vision that attracts committed congregants. Committed members tithe to support the vision, and the church invests those contributions into program and spiritual development, which leads to salvation and people getting their lives changed, which turns into committed members.

Getting churches ready for growth is an important step in preparation for the upcoming harvest of souls. Growing a church takes vision, thought, and strategy. Successful churches are those that follow a God-given vision and map out steps to achieve that vision. The wonder of the body of Christ is that God uses everyone in a slightly different way, and those unique qualities that each church has is what God uses to create a beautiful tapestry in the church world.

Church growth is not about competing with the ministry down the street but more about how God uses the people in the local church and their unique gifts.

I believe people are called to churches for a specific purpose. We are all on a journey, and the church helps us develop as Christians and supports our unique calling.

In his book, Purpose Driven Church, Rick Warren says,

"...[S]ince the church is a living organism, it is natural for it to grow if it is healthy.... [I]f a church is not growing it is dying..."

This can be a scary concept for a small local church. With growth comes many challenges, but the exciting thing is that with God ALL things are possible, and He gives wisdom freely! I have a theory that some churches fail to thrive and grow because the leadership gets comfortable with the way things are and doesn't do anything to change the status quo.

If God called you into ministry, don't take that call lightly. Spend time with Him, and He will instruct you in the way you should go! If you take that instruction, write the vision down, and map out a plan to get there, biblical church growth is inevitable!

About the Author

Patricia Lotich, MBA, is the founder of Smart Church Management and Thriving Small Business. As a business management consultant, Patricia helps organizations put systems and processes in place to manage their limited resources: people, time, and money.

Patricia is also the author of several other books:

Smart Volunteer Management: A Volunteer Coordinator's Handbook for Engaging, Motivating, and Developing Volunteers

Church Staff Evaluations: A Guide to Performance Appraisals that Motivate, Develop, and Reward Church Employees

Church Quality: Why Excellence in the Local Church Is Essential for Growth

Church Job Descriptions: A Collection of 45 Sample Job Descriptions for Church Employees

All books are available on Amazon.

SmartChurchManagement.com

Contact: Info@SmartChurchManagement.com

About Smart Church Management

Smart Church Management (SCM) is a church operations and management consulting company that offers services to help local churches develop systems and processes to support church growth. Whether the system is to manage and budget limited resources recruit, train, and schedule volunteers; or manage the process of hiring, training, and developing church employees, SCM strives to help churches manage their day-to-day operations.

Patricia Lotich, President and CEO of SCM, is an MBA and Certified Manager of Quality and Organizational Excellence through the American Society for Quality. She has ten years of business administration and church operations experience and has a driving passion to help churches fulfill their call by managing the resources God has given them: people, time, and money.

Patricia became a Christian as an adult and has committed to using her business experience and gifts to help the local church. She is an avid (learning) golfer and spends her free time with her husband Bob, lapdog Maggie, and two grown children.

SmartChurchManagement.com

Additional References

Blanchard, K., and Ridge, G., Helping People Win at Work, Polvera Publishing and Garry Ridge, 2009.

Evans, J.R., and Lindsay, W.M., The Management and Control of Quality, South-Western, a division of Thomson Learning, 2002.

Grote, D., The Complete Guide to Performance Appraisal, American Management Association, 1996.

Garrison R., Managerial Accounting, Richard D. Irwin, Inc., 1991, 305-310

LaFasto, F., and Larson C., When Teams Work Best, Sage Publications, 2001.

Heath, D., Heath, C., Made-to-Stick: Why Some Ideas Survive and Others Die, Random House Publishing Group, 2007.

Nelson, B., and Economy, P., Managing for Dummies, Wiley Publishing, Inc., 2003.

Maxwell, J.C., The 21 Irrefutable Laws of Leadership, Maxwell Motivation, Inc., 1998.

Smith, R.D., Strategic Planning for Public Relations, Lawrence Erlbaum Associates, Inc., Publishers, 2002.

Warren, R., The Purpose Driven Church, Zondervan Publishing House, 1995.

Westcott, R.T., The Certified Manager of Quality/ Organizational Excellence, American Society for Quality, Quality Press, Milwaukee 53203, 2006.

https://www.barna.org/congregations-articles/628-the-rise-of-the-pastor

https://www.youtube.com/yt/press/statistics.html

http://www.brotherhoodmutual.com/index.cfm/resources/ministry-safety/article/church-fraud/

http://www.acfe.com/

Additional Resources

To access downloadable copies of forms in this book and for additional resources to help you manage your church, please visit:

SmartChurchManagement.com

61325206R00106

Made in the USA
Middletown, DE
09 January 2018